What The Media Are Saying

Ron Arnold and Alan Gottlieb have money, muscle, and something to say to millions of angry Americans.   —*Outside Magazine*

There's not much you can teach Ron Arnold and Alan Gottlieb about environmental activism. But Arnold and Gottlieb are activists with a difference...   —*People Magazine*

Arnold warned that unless the environmental movement is brought to heel, "public hysteria is going to destroy industrial civilization..." Arnold's organization has published a "wise-use agenda" spelling out an opposing series of goals.   —*The Washington Post*

Mr. Arnold and Mr. Gottlieb say they have borrowed from the early tactics of the environmental movement—newsletters with ominous overtones, direct-mail fund-raising to a very specific audience, the threat of lawsuits— and are just now hitting stride.   —*The New York Times*

The direction of the Center for the Defense of Free Enterprise is determined by two men, Alan Gottlieb and Ron Arnold. Arnold, who confesses to a brief history as a Sierra Club activist, has been described as the movement's "philosopher." Gottlieb, on the other hand, is the money man.   —*Sierra*

The principal organizer of the Wise Use Movement is Alan M. Gottlieb...   —*Harrowsmith Country Life*

Ron Arnold...is gaining increasing national stature and political influence as the arch-druid of the burgeoning movement against environmentalism.   —*The Boston Globe*

Legislatively, Arnold has had a remarkable degree of success. He and Gottlieb organized support for a stringent anti-regulatory bill...   —*Buzzworm: The Environmental Journal*

Alan Gottlieb and Ron Arnold. The two men are the gurus of the Wise Use Movement. Ron Arnold [is] a former Sierra Club activist who has torn whole chapters from the textbook of grass-roots activism...   —*National Parks*

Wise Use has no formal command structure. Any cohesion the movement has comes from a few pivotal figures—notably Ron Arnold [and] Alan Gottlieb...   —*Audubon*

Arnold is now a fixture on the anti-environmental lecture circuit.   —*Greenpeace*

WARNING!: THE ECO-THOUGHT POLICE HAVE DETERMINED THAT READING THIS BOOK MAY BE A VIOLATION OF THE FEDERAL POLITICALLY CORRECT THINKING ACT. STUDIES INDICATE THAT THIS BOOK MAY DRIVE YOU SANE. PROCEED AT YOUR OWN RISK.

Politically Correct Environment

Other books by Alan Gottlieb

The Gun Grabbers
Alan Gottlieb's Celebrity Address Book
Gun Rights Fact Book
The Rights of Gun Owners
Politically Correct Guns
With George Flynn:
Guns for Women
With Ron Arnold: Trashing the Economy
Edited:
The Wise Use Agenda
Fear of Food

Other books by Ron Arnold

At the Eye of the Storm:
James Watt and the Environmentalists
Ecology Wars
The Grand Prairie Years (historical novel)
With Alan Gottlieb: Trashing the Economy
Edited:
Stealing the National Parks
One Man's Life: The Biography of Don Hummel
People of the Tongass
Storm Over Rangelands
The Asbestos Racket
It Takes A Hero
Politically Correct Hunting

Politically Correct Environment

Alan Gottlieb
and
Ron Arnold

cartoons by
Chuck Asay

MERRIL PRESS
BELLEVUE, WASHINGTON

First Edition
Published by Merril Press

Typeset in Century Schoolbook on AMSi computers by Merril
Press, Bellevue, Washington. Cover design by Northwoods
Studio.

Merril Press is an independent publisher and distributor of books
to the trade, P.O. Box 1682,Bellevue, Washington 98009. Telephone 206-455-5038. Fax 206-451-3959. E-mail: Internet:
rarnold@halcyon.com.

This book distributed by Merril Press, P.O. Box 1682, Bellevue,
Washington 98009. Additional copies of this quality paperback
book may be ordered from Merril Press at $14.95 each. Tele-
phone 206-454-7009.

LIBRARY OF CONGRESS CATALOGING-IN-PUBLICATION DATA

Gottlieb, Alan M.
　　Politically correct environment / Alan Gottlieb and Ron
Arnold ; cartoons by Chuck Asay.
　　　　p.　　cm.
　　ISBN 0-936783-15-X
　　1. Environmental protection—Humor. 2. Political correct-
ness—Humor. I. Arnold, Ron. II. Asay, Chuck. III. Title.
PN6231.E66G68　1995
818'.5402—dc20　　　　　　　　　　　　　95-43981
　　　　　　　　　　　　　　　　　　　　　　　CIP

PRINTED IN THE UNITED STATES OF AMERICA
PRINTED ON RECYCLABLE PAPER. WHAT, WE SHOULD KNOW IF IT'S
BEEN RECYCLED ALREADY? WE JUST ORDERED THE CHEAPEST PAPER.

Contents

No dolphins were injured in making this tuna sandwich.

What do you mean this isn't a tuna sandwich?

Dedicated
to all those
who get the jokes

Authors' Preface

"Book 'em, Louie!"

Okay, it's a cliché from a bad movie. But that's what we've done here with all the politically correct environmentalist excesses we live with today.

And even if we can't really arrest the P. C. perpetrators, we can "book 'em" for you in these pages. So consider this the "make sheet" and "mug shot" of all the politically correct environmental wackos we could round up.

Why did we write this little book of gritty gags, saber-tongued stories, irreverent illustrations and zany zingers? Well, the truth is, we just felt like it. But you have to admit that when any subject is elevated to a cultural fetish surrounded by politically correct bowing, scraping and general pussyfooting, it's ripe for parody. When spotted owls and kangaroo rats become more important than people, you *know* it's time to poke a few holes in self-satisfied, holier-than-thou, sanctimonious, smug faced hypocrites everywhere. The environment has become such a sacred cow, somebody just *had* to milk it. So, we elected ourselves chief eco-balloon-bursters, chucklechuckers and idiosyncratic iconoclasts.

We hope *Politically Correct Environment* will become a classic of its type. We designed it as a litmus test. It works like this: Stick your tongue out at this book. If you don't get the jokes, your tongue will turn green, which indicates that you are a Politically Correct Environmentalist. If, on the other hand, you *do* get the jokes, your tongue will not turn green and instead will wiggle in laughter, which indicates you are a Politically Independent Individual. It also indicates the Eco-Thought Police may be knocking at your door some midnight soon.

Any similarity between the stuff in this book and actual persons or events is purely intentional. Our research was done by volunteers in several organizations of Politically Independent Individuals. We would like to thank Americans Against Unconstitutional Government Holdups (A.A.U.G.H.!), End Environmental Nonsense Under Federal Flakes (E.E.N.U.F.F!), and Undo Government Harassment (U.G.H!), for their tireless and tasteless efforts to make this book possible.

Raw material for our jokes supplied by the U. S. Bureau of Really Serious Stupidity and every gag we ever heard. Yes, we know some of them have long beards.

We would like to thank activist Louise Saluteen for the original book concept. We are grateful to Chuck Asay of the Colorado Springs Gazette for permission to reprint his political cartoons.

Now it can be told. Here, then, is *Politically Correct Environment*, the result of at least twenty minutes hard labor.

Have fun.

Alan Gottlieb
Ron Arnold

1
Help! Help!
The Government Is
Taking Over Our Country

The Land of the Free. The Home of the Brave. Apple pie. Motherhood. Forty acres and a mule. Westward, Ho! Pioneering for gold (or spinach, if you're a farmer). Rugged individualism. Family and Community. Self sufficiency. Entrepreneurship. And Industrial Strength. All that stuff.

It built America.

Then came The Environment. The Politically Correct Environment. Laws were passed, court cases fought, bureaucracies created. Now we've got the E.P.A., the U.S.F.S., the B.L.M., N.E.P.A., F.L.P.M.A., C.E.R.C.L.A., T.O.S.C.A. and tons of other alphabet soup shouting, "Stop! You can't do that!" (Doesn't matter what you were doing, it's a ritual government chant.)

Now all that stuff that built America is illegal, immoral or fattening.

Apple pie thickens your middle and makes you a social outcast.

Motherhood is bad—it explodes the population.

Can't use a mule without the mule's written consent because of animal rights.

Can't settle in the West or anywhere else because of Growth Management Acts.

Gold requires mining—ugh!—digging in the *dirt*, a filthy business that ought to be outlawed.

Individual rights? Not a chance. Your right to own property, drive a car, go to work, or conduct your own business must give way to The Public Good, and the public always turns out to be everyone but you.

Family and Community? Are you kidding? If a spotted owl or red cockaded woodpecker or yellow-cheeked warbler lives nearby, bow down in awe, stop farming and ranching and logging and mining and anything else that keeps people alive, then curl up and die. Or else.

Self-sufficiency? No, children, learn to depend on your government so it can protect the environment—trade your resource job for food stamps and retraining vouchers.

The spirit of enterprise and industrial strength? Can't have that, it pollutes. And it keeps people *alive*. Those nasty capitalist products are just selfish *consumerism*. That *uses* things! No! No! Bad human!

It's the law. Environmental law. Politically Correct Environmental law.

It takes power from you. It gives power to the government.

So, it's like we said, the government is taking over our country.

Environmentalists rule.

Well, think about it.

If today's environmental laws had been on the books when we fought the American Revolution, those folks at Concord and Lexington would have had to file a ten-thousand page Environmental Impact Statement before they fired the Shot Heard Round the World. And all that noise! No! No! Bad Minute Man!

General George Washington would have missed the Revolution shopping around New York City and not finding any ivory false teeth—the import ban to stop poaching in Africa, you know. George certainly had the fortitude to stick out winter in Valley Forge, but he was very picky about his choppers.

There couldn't be any Boston or New York City or Philadelphia or Washington, D.C. *or any other city* because aboriginal rights would prevent European settlement and give the land back to the environmentally correct Indians—oops, Native Americans. Got to be politically correct. (But now the Native Americans couldn't use eagle feathers for headdresses or ceremonies because it would endanger the eagles.)

Thomas Jefferson couldn't have written the Declaration of Independence because of all those toxic substances in his ink. And besides, it's politically incorrect to criticize your government. Just ask Bill Clinton. You remember him, don't you?

Abe Lincoln couldn't have been born in a log cabin because the Timber Harvest Plan to cut the trees would have been halted by Ye Olde Sierra Clubbe.

The Washington Monument couldn't be built because the mining permit would be denied to quarry the stone. (Yes, Virginia, that *is too* mining.)

And today, you wouldn't have a place to live: Nobody could build the structure you live in because development involves *habitat destruction,* and that's very, very politically incorrect. (*Human* habitat doesn't count as habitat because environmental law doesn't allow it to count.)

OUT OF WORK AND HUNGRY? EAT AN ENVIRONMENTALIST

(Bumper sticker seen in Alaska)

The government is taking over our country.

Environmentalists rule.

Bureaucrats rule.

Everything is becoming bureaucratean (rhymes with crustacean). Washington, D.C. has turned into the Great Bureaucratean Beast (the collective mass of all bureaus and bureaucrateans).

And the Bureaucratean Beast has a way of biting the hand that feeds it. The E.P.A. will get you if you exhale greenhouse gases. O.S.H.A. will get you leave a paint can open too long. The Corps of Engineers will get you if you fill that rain-soaked sag in your driveway—it's a wetland, and that's a no-no. And the U.S. Fish and Wildlife Service—whoosh! You won't believe what *they'll* do if you so much as twitch.

Consider the marvellous case of Mr. Taung Ming-Lin, for example. He's a wealthy Taiwanese businessman who moved to the United States so he could realize his lifelong dream of being a farmer. Back to the simple life. He'd earned it.

So, Mr. Lin settled in the little California town of South El Monte (no, we never heard of it either) in Kern County. Nice farm country. Mr. Lin bought himself a nice farm.

Then in February 1994, twenty armed state and federal wildlife bureaucrateans descended on Lin's farm and arrested his *tractor*. No kidding. Hauled it away in chains. We're not making this up.

Seems Mr. Lin had made a single pass with his disc to a depth of eight inches, killed five kangaroo rats and disturbed their habitat. That's a violation of the Endangered Species Act. No! No! *Bad* farmer!

The U.S. Fish and Wildlife Service (USFWS) is the agency charged with enforcing the Endangered Species Act (ESA). So, USFWS, with help from

the U.S. Bureau of Stupidity, sought to jail Lin for three years and to fine him $300,000 for farming his land, killing five rats and—omigod!—*disturbing habitat*! They also demanded that he surrender title to 363 acres of the 720 acres he had bought for $1.5 million. And then they demanded that Lin "give" them another $172,425 to run the stolen property as a wildlife preserve. No kidding. We're not making this up.

The local farmers got upset at the government's treatment of a fellow farmer, and held a big rally in front of the federal courthouse in Fresno to protest the outrageous demands of bureacrateans who had lost all sense of proportion. The government didn't like that. No! No! BAD protesters!

In response to this public pressure, the U.S. Fish & Wildlife Service, with aid this time from the U.S. Bureau of Serious Stupidity, raided Lin's offices and threatened his family with deportation. The bureaucrateans then sent the news media a long list of allegations about Lin's background, including claims that he had been jailed in Taiwan, that there was a warrant for his arrest there, and that he was guilty of tax fraud in the United States. All of that turned out to be lies. No kidding. We're not making this up.

DON'T STEAL
THE GOVERNMENT HATES COMPETITION

(Bumper sticker seen in Washington, D.C.)

Then farmers all over America got upset about the government's treatment of Mr. Lin and suggested to Congress that maybe we don't need a U.S. Fish & Wildlife Service, and Senator Larry Craig of Idaho, while smiling at that idea, simply suggested that we ought to take the guns away from all federal bureaucrateans. That really annoyed the government. No! No! *BAD* Senator!

Then the U.S. Fish & Wildlife Service, with aid this time from the U.S. Bureau of Really Serious Stupidity, responded to this public pressure by sending a Frank Kuncir, one of their bureaucrateans, to persuade a local branch of the California Department of Motor Vehicles to suspend Lin's driver's license by claiming that Lin had falsified his license application because his name was misspelled on one of the forms. No kidding. We're not making this up.

What kind of government agency would perpetrate such mean-spirited harassment of people not found guilty of anything?

If it has anything to do with the environment, the answer is: "all of them." They're telling us:

No! No! **BAD** citizens!

Roll over.
Play dead.
The government is taking over our country.

The end of Mr. Lin's story might interest you. In January 1995 the feds dropped their charges against Lin, deciding instead to go after his wife and daughter as officers of his company, which neatly avoided having to answer in court for their campaign of lies and disinformation to assassinate the character of Mr. Lin. But they didn't want to face a jury trial, and when it became clear they couldn't avoid one, they gave up.

Not because they realized they were wrong. Because they realized they couldn't win in a fair fight.

Mr. Lin agreed in a settlement to donate a $5,000 blackmail payment to a habitat conservation fund, but he admits no wrongdoing. His land will remain unfarmed, but the feds have promised to stop trying to seize it.

Mr. Lin has not been found guilty of anything, but he had to give the bureaucrateans a payoff and he can't farm his own land.

No kidding. We're not making this up.

The government is taking over our country.
The Land of the Free.
Roll over.
The Home of the Brave.
Play dead.
The Land of Politically Correct Environment.
Curl up and die.

Well, if the government is taking over our country, what do we do about it? Roll over? Play dead? Curl up and die?

Naaah.

We could have a little fun by making the bureaucrateans live up to their own rules. Just the other day we spotted a U.S. Department of Energy vehicle on the freeway with a *single occupant*. That just won't do, not after all those DOE lectures we've listened to about car pooling and public transit. Let's limit bureaucrateans to buses, van pools, and bicycles. Let's afflict them with the same regulations they inflict on us. Is that fair?

It's a start, anyway.

FRIENDS DON'T LET FRIENDS BECOME A SIERRA CLUBBER

Bumper sticker seen stuck to a hiking trail sign.

And when we howled a little about government abuses, Bill Clinton told us to shut up and stop hating the government. Yo, Bill! This is America. We *are* the government. We don't hate government. We just don't like bureaucratic abuses.

We'd like to look forward to a morning cup of coffee without some bureaucratean swimming in it.

And has anybody repealed that little item in Amendment One about petitioning for redress of grievances? Or did we miss something somewhere?

Presidents shouldn't take themselves too seriously. Nobody else does.

Government, we work for a living, we send you our taxes, we fight your wars, we make our country great and we love the environment because we live in it and we work in it. Is it too much to ask that you quit biting our hand and that you learn to act like a good neighbor?

We guess our motto should be: **Help Starve A Feeding Bureaucrat**.

And somebody has to revive Lord Acton's levelheaded reminder about absolute power and say:

No! No! *BAD* government!

2
Enviro-Speak:
A Dictionary of Eco-Babble

You can't tell the players without a scorecard. You can't get the jokes unless you know the vocabulary. To the Politically Correct Environmentalist, words don't mean the same as they do to you and me.

Enviro-Speak words that describe the environment are surrounded by a halo of warm fuzzy feelgood emotions. Enviro-Speak words that describe human beings, the economy, or using the earth for anything at all are etched in acid tones of venom, fear and contempt.

And then there's Bureaucratean, the mother tongue of Enviro-Speak, a language steeped in acronyms, alphabet soup and pretentious circumlocutions designed to avoid clear statement.

We have striven to include the most useful words in Enviro-Speak and Bureaucratean, defined here with perfect clarity and absolute precision.

Remember our motto: Eschew obfuscation!

Acton's law: Power tends to corrupt, and absolute power corrupts absolutely. [John, Lord Acton (1834-1902), first modern philosopher of resistance to the evil state, whether its form be authoritarian, democratic or socialist. Politically Correct Environmentalist power, on the other hand, purifies. You believe that, don't you?] **(Acton's breakfast: ham and eggs.)**

American Dream: 1. The environmental nightmare from which we must awaken. 2. What people achieve when government gets the hell out of the way.

American way of life: 1. Nasty, greedy, corrupt, consumerist, shallow, pathetic, anxiety-ridden, ignorant, violent, drug-addicted, exploiting, polluting, decadent, stinking cesspool of a rat race. 2. Opportunity, risk-taking, reward, responsibility; often associated with hard work, ingenuity, and persistence.

Animal companion: Preferred name for a pet. People for the Ethical Treatment of Animals insists it is demeaning to an animal to be owned by a human, which is animal slavery.

Animal Liberation Front: Underground ecowarriors that protect critters under the motto, "Don't use animals for anything or we will kill you." Made it to the FBI's Top Ten Domestic Terrorist List after lots of bombings, arsons and attempted murders. Targets humans who believe they are superior to animals and have the right to enslave, experiment upon and eat animals. Violent Vegetarians.

Animal rights: 1. A movement to rewrite the Constitution to say, "We the Animals...." 2. Front group for the vegetable industry.

Anthropocentric, anthropocentrism: Environmentalist theory that says humans are bad because we look at the world from our own viewpoint.

Biocentric, biocentrism: Environmentalist theory that says humans should see the center of existence as all life except human life.

Bioregionalism: Demand to replace nations with "bioregions"—ecosystems rather than political boundaries. Humans must abandon civilization and adhere to the needs of their bioregion rather than impose their technology upon nature.

Biosphere: Large spherical place for everything to live in except people.

BIOSPHERE

Biosphere Preserves: 1. Jam made from the biosphere. 2. United Nations nature preserve program to declare all areas of the Earth out of bounds for human use.

botanical companion: a plant, from algae to trees.

botanical companion embracer: tree hugger.

Buncombe, Edward: Died in the Revolutionary War after his name became synonymous with hot air (see **global warming**). His name evolved into "bunkum" and then just plain "bunk." Patron saint of environmental lobbyists.

bureaucrat: Public servant who knows how to run your life better than you, and insists upon proving it.

bureaucratean: (rhymes with crustacean) *adjective*: relating to or describing the appearance, activity and mind-style of the genus Bureaucratia. *noun*: an individual member of that genus, i.e., a bureaucrat.

Bureaucratean Beast: The genus Bureaucratia considered as a whole. The sum total of all bureaucratic agencies. Feeds on taxes. Bites taxpayer hands. Thinks the environment is more important than the taxpayers who pay to protect it.

Bureaucratia: (rhymes with crustacea) Family of hominids known for their blundering gait, low foreheads and characteristic seeking for the hardest way to do an easy job when protecting the environment.

building code enforcement: You did it my way. If my way's the wrong way, it's your problem.

capitalist: 1. Person whose sole products are pollution, destruction of the environment, enslavement of employees and political oppression. 2. Source of funds that support those who believe 1.

cities: buildings and other infrastructure that take up room needed for restoring **ecosystems** (see **ecosystem** entry).

civilization: Environmental disaster that allows humans to increase in number by applying technology to nature to increase its outputs of food, fiber, minerals and all other material goods.

cockroach: animal companion resembling environmental organizations when confronted with their financial records. Eco-groups run from the light when the public is shown how wealthy they are, that a lot of their money comes from polluting industries, and that many receive government grants.

dams: fish killers that must be removed.

deep ecology: Deep science of saving deep nature by putting shallow people six feet deep. Similar to vast ecology and half-vast ecology.

degraded: Land which has been farmed, grazed, logged, built on or otherwise used by humans.

dolphin safe: 1) a big metal vault where dolphins keep their important papers.

Earth First!: Practical environmental group that seeks to restore ecosystems by burning, blowing up, smashing or otherwise destroying civilization. Advocated "tree spiking" to deter loggers and millworkers by "inoculating" trees with hard objects that would break sawblades on contact and fill the air with deadly shrapnel. Earth First! shoots livestock to bankrupt ranchers, blows up heavy equipment to stop loggers and miners, sabotages power lines to disrupt everyone. Earth First!, People Last!

ecology: Science of hitching everything to everything else, using red tape first and ending with chains.

ecofeminism: movement that says patriarchal oppressor societies are the cause of all environmental degradation because women in peaceful matriarchal societies would have executed all the technologists if they had political power.

ecosystem: Natural environment without human degradation. Condition to which degraded lands must be returned.

ecosystem management: 1. Bureaucratean technique of managing government lands by doing absolutely nothing with them and getting paid for it. 2. Scientific-sounding excuse to remove all commodity production activities from federal lands.

ecotage: Sabotage of human artifacts to protect nature. Dave Foreman's ecotage instruction manual, *Ecodefense: A Field Guide to Monkeywrenching,* says ecotage is to be done without hurting any human being. Captain Paul Watson's *Earthforce! An Earth Warrior's Guide to Strategy* has its doubts, and says "strategy by nature is a martial discipline." Screaming Wolf's *A Declaration of War: Killing People to Save Animals and the Environment* says just kill 'em.

ecowarrior: One who performs ecotage, sometimes called an "ecoteur" or "ecodefender" but never an "ecoterrorist" because the loggers and miners and farmers and fishers are the real ecoterrorists.

environment: Every place except where people live. **(environmental disaster:** Where people live.)

Environmental Defense Fund: Little Washington, D.C. environmental group with a $17 million annual budget and an executive director named Fred Krupp who pulls down $193,558 in salary and $17,216 in benefits. Think of all those $25 donations it takes to pay the boss. Registered as a public *charity*.

Environmental Grantmakers Association: a cartel of big-money foundations with their own "progressive" social agendas that control the funding and programs of many environmental groups such as the National Audubon Society, the Nature Conservancy and the Wilderness Society.

Environmental Thought Police: Self-appointed gaggle of oxymorons, harvardmorons and yalemorons.

environmentalism: 1. Belief system holding that 1) Nature is terribly fragile; 2) Anything people do hurts Nature; 3) There is no hope for Nature unless people stop doing things; 4) A few of us will tell the rest of you when and how to stop doing things; 5) If you don't stop doing things, Nature will come to an end, and then you'll be sorry, won't you? (see entry under **gloom and doom**.) 2. A government careers program for those who can't make it in the private sector.

environmentalist: One who knows the value of everything, but the price of nothing.

gloom and doom: 1. The Environmentalist's Creed. 2. Primary output of environmental organizations. 3. Secret ingredient of environmentalist fund raising.

environmental law: Legal system designed to prohibit _____.
(your project here)

farmers: 1. Country hicks who pollute groundwater with pesticides and synthetic fertilizers, erode the soil with gas-guzzling tractors, poison consumers with contaminated products and care about nothing but chasing a dollar. 2. People who feed and clothe those who believe 1.

federal government: Command central of the genus Bureaucratia, control center for environmentalists who want to run your life. Works on the principle, "The farther from home you send your tax money, the harder of hearing it gets."

federal lands: 1. What "public" lands really are, a fact environmentalists hide because it sounds too much like government. 2. The private property of the federal government. No trespassing.

free enterprise: An unfashionable reliance upon individual decisions in the marketplace based on competition. Too disorderly for environmentalists.

Freedom of Information Act: 1. *What the law says:* If the government won't tell you, use the Freedom of Information Act. 2. *What the bureaucratean says:* If you have to ask, you're not entitled to know. 3. *What really happens:* You have to sue the bureaucratean to make him/her/it follow the law.

Friends of the Earth: A little $2.4 million Washington, D.C. eco-group that acts like the Enemies of the People by complaining about every productive enterprise on Earth.

global cooling: 1970s prediction of a catastrophic return of the Ice Age. When the glaciers failed to bury New York City, environmental groups failed to bury themselves in money from donors and the scam was abruptly dumped in favor of:

global warming: Hot air from Politically Correct Environmentalist propaganda.

globaloney: Anything an environmentalist says about a world crisis.

Gottlieb's Law of Pollution: One man's pollution is another man's raw material.

government: 1. Us (theoretical principle). 2. (Practical definition): Those public servants in Washington, D.C. who serve us—medium rare, after a process during which we are first carved and then roasted.

government assistance: Program designed to replace productive employment in resource industries, based on the premise, "I can fence any animal I can get to take a free handout."

greenhouse gases: Hot air emanating from an environmentalist's house. (See **global warming**.)

Greenpeace: Leading door-to-door solicitors for saving this and that. Their combined American branches take in about $48 million a year. They used some of their big bucks to end the seal skin fur trade and destroy the lives of indigenous peoples in the Arctic. Very green. Very peaceful.

hiking: Sole human activity tolerated in ecosystems.

home: Occupied environmental disaster area.

homeless: Those who live in the environment.

human beings: The worst, nastiest environmental disaster ever to hit Planet Earth. They eat, they shit, they breed, they *use* things. Unless eliminated, they'll be the end of nature. See illustration (right) of properly nourished human being.

illions: Counting system of bureaucrateans. Once began with "M," gradually evolved to "B," now spelled with a "T," developing into "Z."

industry: 1. Complex whose sole function is that of polluter of the air and water, raper of the land, destroyer of the Earth. 2. Firms, employees and communities that provide all material goods to those who believe 1.

legislation by headline: art of convicting any industry of being an environmental criminal by feeding scare stories to the media, neatly avoiding the need to convince Congress or state legislatures that you are right. Uses the **might of environmentalism** (see entry) to undermine America's industrial might.

logger: 1. Destroyer of forests who goes into the woods each morning and randomly chops down every tree in sight, breaks them into little pieces and crushes the bits into the dirt with a bulldozer, causing massive erosion and desertification, all for the sheer meanness of it. 2. Person who provides shelter, photographic film and writing paper to those who believe 1.

might of environmentalism, the: Environmental organizations' use of the word *"might"* when talking about an eco-crisis: "A million children *might* die from Alar on apples;" or "Global warming *might* occur if we don't ban the automobile;" or "The last tree in the world *might* be cut if we don't stop timber harvest in Poverty Gulch, New Mexico." A way to scare the public without really saying anything.

mineral companions: Jewels. Just as animal companions remind us of animal rights and botanical companions remind us of veggie rights, mineral companions teach us about mineral rights. Mineral companions are a girl's best friend.

mitigation: What happens to the gate in your fence when a bureaucratean hits it with a baseball catcher's glove.

monkeywrenching: Sabotage of any equipment used in logging, mining, farming, or construction, done by brave ecodefenders (anonymously, of course).

multiple use: Two environmentalists hiking in the same wilderness area during the same year.

Murphy's Law of Ecology: If anything can go wrong, environmentalists will prove it's your fault.

National Audubon Society: Washington, D.C. eco-activist group that used to watch birds but now puts working people out of jobs with its $40 million budget and a former president named Peter Berle who took $178,000 in salary and $21,285 in benefits as his cut from public donations to save the birds.

National Register of Hysterical Sights: Government list of really funny looking places.

National Wildlife Federation: Tiny little Washington, D.C. environmental group with a budget of $82 million and a former executive director named Jay Hair who got $242,060 in salary, $34,155 in benefits and an expense account of $23,661. Registered as a public charity. Go figure.

nationalization: What environmentalists do with your property, your rights and your freedoms.

Nature: A PBS show about cute little animals. It tells us olives have feelings. Tomatoes are people too.

natural: Pristine pre-European condition to which degraded land must be restored.

Natural Resources Defense Council: Created by the Ford Foundation to mug business and industry, still funded at $20 million a year from grants and members. Created the Alar scam (Alar is a growth regulator substance once used to keep apples from ripening too soon) that bankrupted thousands of innocent apple orchardists through accusations that Alar causes cancer in children—never proven. NRDC executive John H. Adams gets $145,526 salary and $13,214 benefits from donations.

naturalist: The most natural you can get.

Nature Conservancy: Champion nationalizer of private land. With its $278 million income, it buys private land at lowball prices and sells it to the government above appraised value. Gets $28 million a year in government taxpayer grants. Their fund raising ads call this "Conservation through private action." The Conservancy pays president John Sawhill $185,000 salary and $17,118 in benefits, which actually is private action.

Plant Rights Movement: Legal standing for veggies. Onions have feelings. Soybeans are people too. Vegetarianism is murder! No sobriety tests for stewed tomatoes! Free medical treatment for mashed potatoes! Cotton looks better in its own boll!

population control: Environmentalist goal to bring the human population down to the carrying capacity of the Earth, which is calculated by eco-experts to be three people: Mom, Dad, and the Population Controller, who makes sure they don't reproduce.

private property: 1. Temporary land occupancy of no value by people of no value, but envied by an environmentalist, who wants the government to take it without paying for it. 2. That stuff the Fifth Amendment mentions in passing.

public lands: 1. Government lands that belong to all of us except for the people who live there. 2. Private property of the federal government. No trespassing.

Sierra Club: A blunt instrument used to put working people in the unemployment line. Its $41 million budget gives it the clout to whammy loggers, miners, ranchers, farmers and fishermen to death. Its sister-outfit, the Sierra Club Legal Defense Fund rakes in another $9.5 million, mostly from taking people to court, and pays executive director Vawter Parker $106,507 in salary and $10,650 in benefits.

rainforest: Any forest where an environmentalist doesn't want you to cut trees. Prefixing the word "rain" to the naked word "forest" promotes mystical reverence. First there were tropical rainforests to stop all logging in the tropics, then temperate rainforests to stop all logging in temperate climates, and now we are hearing of desert rainforests, deep sea rainforests, lunar rainforests, and interstellar rainforests, to keep people away from every place in the universe.

rancher: 1. Raper of the earth who uses cows and sheep to devastate rangelands, making cows drink a ton of water to make a pound of beef, making sheep pull the grass up by the roots, and causing global warming by release of greenhouse gases from cow farts. 2. Person who provides food, fiber and shoeleather to those who believe 1.

recycle: Technological marvel to make stuff go away and come back as something else. Invented in ancient Mesopotamia by junk metal traders offering new lamps for old.

regulation: Government control of private property, private rights and private liberties to provide free goods to the public.

Skpetic's First Question: Did you ever see an environmentalist smile?

Skeptic's Second Question: Really? Who died?

social change: Coins given out by the government from someone else's pocket.

speciesism: An environmentally correct term that deplores human beings who think they are superior to animals and plants. In order to be non-speciesist, humans must give full legal rights to every species, particularly non-cute species such as warthogs, flatworms, slime molds, amoebas and viruses (see illustration, right). Humans must also stop eating other species. Other species, however, are not similarly constrained, such as the virus shown.

sustainable development: 1. A government program making applicants prove they can do something forever before giving them a permit to do it for a little while. 2. A way to misdirect attention away from the fact that economic growth is not part of the program.

takings: 1. **direct takings**: Government saving the environment by confiscating private property under the legal theory, "What's mine is mine; what's yours is negotiable." 2. **regulatory takings**: Government saving the environment by regulation that forbids economic use of private property under the same theory.

tree-spiking: ecodefense method involving the insertion of metal or undetectable hard plastic spikes in trees to cause kickback of chainsaws and resultant injury of loggers. Prime example of the ecodefender's prohibition against harming human life while sabotaging human artifacts.

Turtle Island: What some indigenous peoples used to call the continent of North America. A phrase now used by environmentalists to show their contempt for the society that gave them birth, educated them, and taught them the indigenous meaning of the phrase "Turtle Island," which was never written in Native American histories because those cultures did not possess written language.  Turtle Island is shown here with the artificial political boundaries of the invader cultures, not the indigenous bioregions. Map by satellite not invented by Turtles.

urban sprawl: humans living on private land outside high-density cities where planners want them.

Voluntary Human Extinction Movement, or VHEMNT (pronounced "vehement"): Plan dreamed up by Earth First! founder Dave Foreman to evacuate the Planet. Vehement environmentalists approved the idea, but none volunteered to show us how it's done.

Washington, D.C.: 1. Nation's capital. Babylon on the Potomac. 2. Ten square miles of politicians surrounded by stark reality. Inside the Beltway, perception is reality. Outside the Beltway, reality is reality.

Wetland: 1. Any private property where rain has fallen at any time during the past billion years. Includes Timbuktu in the Sahara Desert, Alice Springs in the Australian Outback and the top of the Empire State Building. Human use is punishable by confiscation of property, fine and imprisonment. 2. A swamp.

wild and scenic rivers: vacant riverside lots where homes were removed to create open space for canoe and kayak enthusiasts.

wilderness: 1. a state of mind that wipes out all awareness of human beings and goes psychotic if evidence of human activity appears anywhere in the same landscape. 2. a place where environmentalists flock to share solitude. 3. resources that have been saved so future generations can't use them either.

Wilderness Society: Purist eco-group with a $16 million budget that stops everyone else from logging, but whose president, John Roush, clearcut his private forest in Montana right up to the boundary of the adjoining National Forest. The Wilderness Society's multimillion dollar investment portfolio also contained stock in Caterpillar (bulldozer manufacturer) and Cummins Engine (manufacturer of diesel engines used in bulldozers). Money is not important to the Wilderness Society. Well, *your* money is not important to the Wilderness Society, unless it's in a donation check written to their account.

World Wildlife Fund: International eco-group whose American branch has a $60 million budget and an executive director, Kathryn Fuller, who gets $185,000 salary and $16,650 in benefits. What's left over pays for staff wildlife.

3
Correct / Incorrect

How can the average American stay politically correct about the environment?

The truth is, you can't.

It's too self-righteous, snooty and hifalutin for most of us.

But let's give it a shot.

First, read all the popular books on the subject. You know, titles like *50 Weird Things You Absolutely Must Do To Save The Earth*, or *How To Survive The Coming End Of The World*, or *Now You Can Stop Breathing And Start Being Environmentally Correct*.

We know it's not easy, what with all the eco-babble of Enviro-Speak to cope with, so we've taken this chapter to give you concrete examples—oops, that sounds too much like pavement—let's make that *specific illustrations* of what's hip and what's not.

Politically Correct Farm Poster Contest
Losing Entry

Politically Correct Farm Poster Contest
Winning Entry

We don't need
farmers
where I live
because
there's a
Safeway
right across
the street

Politically Incorrect Sovereignty

I pledge allegiance...

Politically Correct Sovereignty

My Bioregion,
right or wrong!

Politically Incorrect
Botanical Companions

Forest
(sounds ordinary)

Politically Correct
Botanical Companions

Rainforest
(sounds awesome)

Politically Incorrect
Geographic Orientation

We all live upstream
So let's act responsibly

Politically Correct
Geographic Orientation

We all live downstream
So let's act like victims

Politically Incorrect
Food Distribution

Oppressor Species
Starve to reduce population
No dolphins were injured in drawing this cartoon.

Politically Correct
Food Distribution

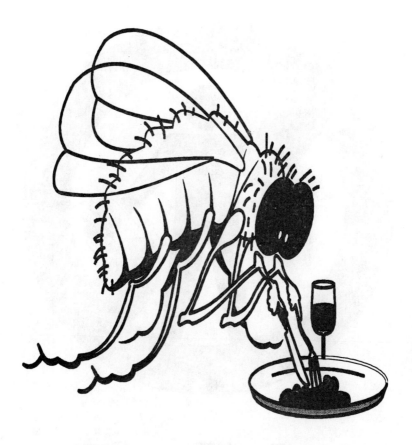

Victim Species
Feed to increase population

Politically Incorrect

How Red-Tape Cutter
Feels About E.P.A.

Politically Correct

How E.P.A. Feels About
Red-Tape Cutter

See what we mean?

There's no way the average American can stay politically correct about the environment.

But now you have the experience necessary to go on to the meat of the book—oops, *meat* sounds too much like an oppressor species anti-animal remark—to the heart of the book—no, that sounds too much like meat—to the guts of the book—no, *that* sounds too much like meat!

Oh, hell, you know what we mean.

You're ready for the next tasty chapter.

Lick your chops.

4
Be Environmental Or Else

The Politically Correct Environment motto: Government knows best.

The Bureaucratean Beast smacks its lips every time a hapless citizen applies for permission to do something a free person would not have to ask permission to do, like build an addition to his or her own home. You're just another tasty morsel to be chewed up and spit out by Bureaucratia.

The list of outrages committed by the Bureaucratean Beast against the ordinary citizen is too long to put between the covers of any book, but we've selected a typical cross-section.

What better way to laugh at our adversities than in political cartoons? Chuck Asay's inspired jabs at Bureaucratia tell our story perfectly.

Compliance Assistance Officers

The U. S. Environmental Protection Agency calls its enforcement personnel "Compliance Assistance Officers."

If you are a farmer and you hire a crop duster to spray insecticide on your vegetable row crops, a team of Compliance Assistance Officers equipped with automatic weapons will arrest your tractor and haul you and your tractor off in chains.

If you are a rancher and you fence off your stock watering pond so that wild donkeys can't drink your water before your cows get to it, a team of Compliance Assistance Officers equipped with automatic weapons will arrest your horse and you and haul you both off in leg restraints.

If you are a small timberlands owner and you cut a tree down in your own private forest, a team of Compliance Assistance Officers equipped with automatic weapons will arrest your chainsaw and you and haul you both off tied up in logging cable.

If you are a miner and you break a rock while exploring for molybdenum or cobalt or some other industrial mineral, a team of Compliance Assistance Officers equipped with automatic weapons will arrest your geologist's hammer and you and haul you both off snarled in red tape.

If you are a President who's really serious about helping Bureaucratean Compliance Assistance Officers, you will look like the cartoon on the right.

A famous cartoon by Chuck Asay, "Huntin' Camp Photo," became so popular it was reprinted by dozens of wise use grassroots activists. Yeah, us too. To view cartoon turn book sideways. Yes, you heard us: *sideways*. Come on, don't be difficult. You need the exercise anyway.

Cumulative Regulatory Impact

Be a model citizen. Obey all laws.

You can follow this sound advice in everything except environmental law.

Congress, in its infinite wisdom (and its infinite ability to write an infinitely large number of laws) has not paid much attention to what Bureaucratia does with the many environmental laws it writes.

It is the Bureaucratean Beast's duty to promulgate regulations that set forth a suitable method of enforcing the laws that Congress writes.

The trouble is, Bureaucratia has no incentive to do things simply. The more regulations Bureaucratia promulgates to enforce a simple law, the more personnel, appropriations and clout it gets from Congress. Congress is supposed to rein in Bureaucratia through "Oversight Committees," but by an oversight, oversight becomes an oversight.

Pretty soon the regulations are so tangled from one law to another nobody can figure out what they mean, much less follow them.

The result is, if you obey Regulation #1 to the letter, that is likely to cause you to violate Regulation #2, which will invoke Regulation #3, so a bureaucratean will have to promulgate Regulation #4 to solve the conflict. The lawsuits generated by this confusion will result in Regulation #5.

Chuck Asay's cartoon tells it all.

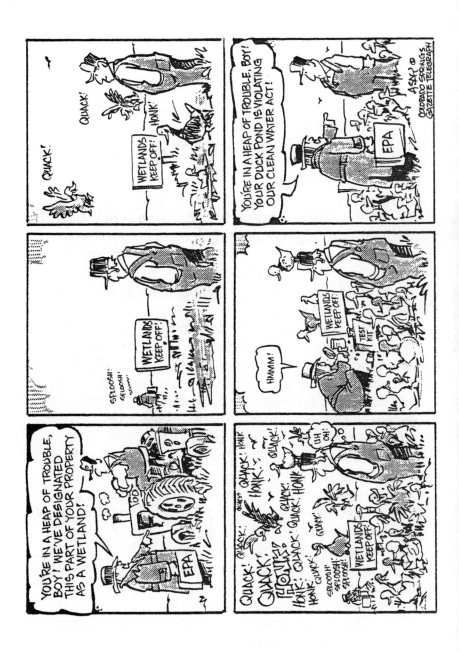

Private Property

A man's home is his castle.

A woman's home is her castle.

Except in the Politically Correct Environment.

Environmentalists insist that humans are merely a passing phase in the evolution of life on Earth, and that the property of humans is not theirs at all, but merely a temporary loan of resources that belong to the public of all generations, past, present and future. Your title to the land means nothing. The property ownership system itself is evil and ought to be abolished.

So, you're just the steward of your land, a temporary caretaker with no rights. You can't use your land without permission of the public. Of course, you must pay taxes on the land you can't use. The public has to be supported by somebody, and the property owner should be punished for the unfair advantage of owning property.

Everything in PC Environment Land is held in trust for the public. The public, of course, is everyone except you. Eco-thieves call this the Public Trust Doctrine. The public gets your land and you trust the public not to jail you as long as you pay your taxes and stay off your land.

It is the Bureaucratean Beast's goal to create public rights to private property. The Beast's motto is, "It doesn't have to make sense."

The Asay cartoon explains some recent international history of property rights.

The National Biological Service

How would you like the government to come prowling around your home without your knowledge or permission, write down everything living in your yard, see if it's on one of their endangered species lists and then tell you, "Sorry, you can't live here anymore, we have to protect the endangered lesser louseplant and the bloated humbug." Hmm?

If you like that, you'll love the National Biological Service. It's a bureaucracy dreamed up by environmentalists for one reason only: To control all the private property in America.

The National B.S., as dissidents call it, began life as the National Biological Survey, a project to identify and locate every living thing in America. When Congress killed the proposal, Interior Secretary Bruce Babbitt kept it alive anyway, sneaking it into the Department of the Interior and using slush funds to keep it going.

Babbitt renamed it the National Biological Service. You know why the government calls a bureaucracy a "service," don't you? It's a farming term. When you need to have your cow freshened, you take her to a stud farm to have her serviced by a bull.

Now we have the National Biological Service, servicing a whole nation of unsuspecting home owners. Take that, American citizen! Just relax, baby, you'll learn to like it in time.

Eco-Cops

The Green Helmets are coming! The Green
Helmets are coming!

Never heard of them?

Keep mowing your lawn and you will. Or keep
exhaling carbon dioxide, that nasty greenhouse gas.

The Green Helmets are a global environmental police force dreamed up by French environmentalist, Dr. Jacques-Yves Cousteau, better known for
his documentaries of the oceans filmed from his research ship, *Calypso*.

In the Cousteau Society's newsletter, *Calypso
Log,* of February 1992, Cousteau wrote, "Here I am
referring to the necessity of creating an international
environmental police, 'green helmets,' who would be
under the direction of the United Nations. Our planet
needs guardians, independent organizations, free of
the constraints of profit or national sovereignty, and
responsible for making up an almost daily bill of
health of our common habitat, our Earth."

Hmm... Free of the constraints of national sovereignty... Yes, um-hmm. And these people will have
guns, right?

So far, Cousteau's eco-cops haven't been issued
their combat gear. The U.N. ain't cooperating. Yet.

But the Environmental Protection Agency
makes up for it here in the U.S. with their swat teams
sent out to make life miserable for that ugly greedy
polluter, the American citizen.

Foundations

We usually think of foundations as those nice people who give money to childrens' hospitals, homeless shelters, the civic opera and college scholarships for deserving underprivileged students.

But today the non-profit sector, fueled by foundation money, makes up more than ten percent of the total U.S. economy. And a big chunk of foundation cash goes to funding environmental groups.

The hottest activist foundations, the Rockefeller Family Fund (Standard Oil money), the Pew Charitable Trusts (Sun Oil money), the W. Alton Jones Foundation (Citgo Oil money) and a bunch of others, formed the Environmental Grantmakers Association to give over $300 million a year to eco-groups. That's a tidy sum.

These foundations get their vast annual income from professionally managed investment portfolios. They invest mostly in Fortune 500 Big Money corporations. But the foundations are very liberal, wanting to redistribute the wealth to their favorite charities.

Why would big money outfits do that? Try this on for size: If you're a big well capitalized industry, why wouldn't you give millions every year to a superlobby that passes laws so strict that only big well capitalized industries can afford to comply with them? You wouldn't mind getting rid of the medium-sized and small competition, would you?

And the foundations want to redistribute the wealth to their favorite charities because they control their favorite charities. Hmmm....

We're From the Twilight Zone

The story of David Lucas is instructive. We don't know what the lesson is, but it's instructive.

In 1986 David bought two nice beachfront properties on the South Carolina coast, dreaming of building a home for his family on one and a home for sale on the other.

But in 1988, the state legislature passed a law enabling the South Carolina Coastal Commission to draw setback lines along the coast, seaward of which no structures could be built. You can see it coming. David Lucas was greenlined out of his dream home. The government told him he could not build on the lots he owned, but he could continue to pay taxes on them.

This ticked him off. He sued the commission for an unconstitutional taking of his land and the jury awarded him $1.23 million. However, the state supreme court reversed the lower court.

David took his case to the U.S. Supreme Court, where he won a ruling that the state had indeed taken his land unconstitutionally. The high court sent the case back to the state supreme court, which duly ruled that Lucas had been unlawfully deprived of his land and ordered him compensated.

The state accordingly paid for and acquired David Lucas's two beachfront lots.

The state didn't want to keep the two lots, so it decided to sell them—for development.

Go figure. Ta-tee-ta-ta, Ta-tee-ta-ta.

Trashing the Economy

Environmental wackos love the environment, right? And they don't really want to hurt the economy, right?

Then why did Portland, Oregon-based environmental activist Randall O'Toole tell *Newsweek* in the September 30, 1991 issue (p. 62) that "cumulatively, the environmental movement is interested in shutting down the timber industry." Hmm?

Somehow, doesn't it seem that shutting down the timber industry might hurt the economy? Just a teensy bit?

And environmental wackos really love the spotted owl, don't they? And they really just want to protect it, don't they? And that's all they were trying to do when they shut down the timber industry in the Pacific Northwest, wasn't it?

Then why did Sierra Club Legal Defense Fund analyst Andy Stahl tell an environmental law conference, "When it comes to protecting old growth, I've often thought that thank goodness the spotted owl evolved, for if it hadn't, we'd have to genetically engineer it. It's a perfect species to use as a surrogate."

And they used this kind of thinking to put 30,000 forest workers in the unemployment line! Eco-freak Andy Kerr called the loggers "collateral damage."

What's the difference between bank robbers and environmentalists?

Bank robbers steal from folks who HAVE money.

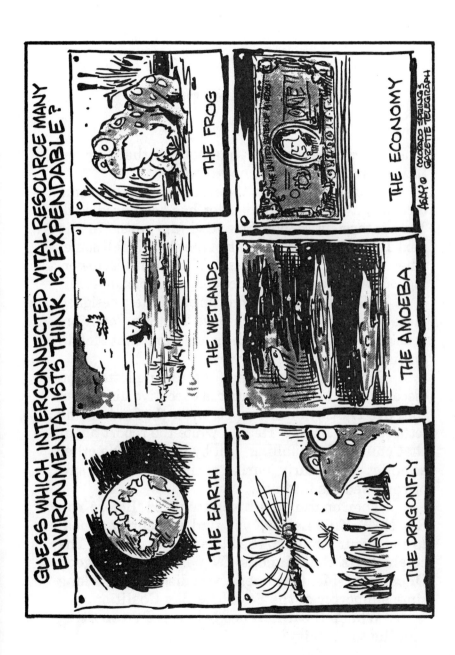

The Sky Is Falling

By now everybody has noticed the Chicken Little Syndrome. Here's how it works:

You see a report on the evening news that some terrible environmental disaster has been predicted. They interview Melvin Scientist who says, "In the next 100 years, a large chunk of the sky will fall somewhere in the United States." The TV interviewer, Isgood Oncamera, clucks her tongue deploringly.

A few days later, you get an elaborately designed piece of junk mail from the Save The Sky Coalition. It asks for money. It says the same thing that Melvin Scientist told the TV interviewer.

But at the end of the fund raising letter, you discover that Melvin Scientist is executive director of the Save The Sky Coalition. He wrote the fund raising letter in your hands. He also wrote the report about that chunk of sky falling. All by himself. No other scientist or scholarly journal or institution ever saw or reviewed his findings.

Then on the little brochure titled "Before You Say No To This Letter," you find a celebrity appeal to send your money to the Save The Sky folks. The celebrity is that famous TV personality, Isgood Oncamera. Ms. Oncamera, you discover, is a long time supporter of the Save The Sky Coalition.

What's the difference between TV reporting and the tooth fairy?

The tooth fairy is real.

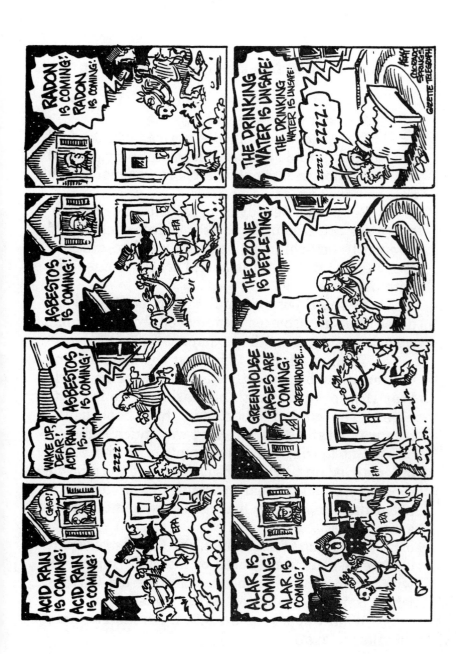

False Alarms and True Alarms

Asbestos causes cancer!

The headline stunned America. Think of all the things that had asbestos in them. Why, a lot of the insulation in our public schools was made with that wonder mineral, asbestos!

But people were dying of asbestos-induced cancer years after being exposed. Think what would happen to our children, being exposed to asbestos every school day in those horrid school rooms filled with asbestos!

So the Environmental Protection Agency ordered that all asbestos be removed from all public schools at the cost of the taxpayer.

Then, it came to light that the people dying of cancer had been mostly shipfitters during World War II who worked with blue asbestos to insulate pipes. The kind of asbestos in the school insulation was totally different, and was much safer.

But tearing it out to comply with the E.P.A. order stirred up a lot of asbestos dust, and the removal contractors had to wear spacesuit-like protection to avoid the danger they had caused by removing the asbestos.

Speaking of spacesuits, the Challenger space shuttle disaster was caused by faulty O rings made with a non-asbestos substitute for the old O rings, which contained asbestos. E.P.A. orders.

What happens to an E.P.A. bureaucrat when he takes a laxative?

He disappears.

Media Bias

My expert's better than your expert.

It's a lawyer's game as old as the shills. The plaintiff, Acey Soap Company, hires scholarly Dr. Verien Telekshull, who wrote the text book on *zuk*, a secret ingredient in laundry soap, which they claim was stolen by their competitor, defendant Deucy Soap Company. So the lawyer for Deucy hires flashy Dr. Nowit Awhl, a famous science popularizer, and he mops the floor with stodgy Dr. Telekshull during cross examination. Dr. Awhl tells the jury in homey style that any bright lab technician could find a substitute for zuk, and that Deucy had done it legally. Dr. Telekshull testifies for an hour in scientific jargon, proving that such a substitute does not exist, and that Deucy stole zuk. The jury believes the slick popularizer. Deucy wins.

It doesn't matter who's right, it just matters who can convince the jury best.

The media borrowed the game and added a few refinements of their own.

The key is to focus the cameras madly on your favorite expert for the entire time slot and then yank the microphone away from the expert you don't agree with. Sorry, out of time.

If you can't keep the expert you hate off the air, make sure you catch him off guard with footage showing him shooing away a fly or picking his nose. Edit that in while you show him on screen. Makes him look very "convincing."

Individual Liberties
and Permission Slips

Give me government or give me death!

Ask any environmentalist. Patrick Henry might not have said it *exactly* that way, but you get the idea. We the People are so BAD for the environment we need governing down to the last detail.

We the People? Naah. Now it's We the Bureaucrats. Pursuit of happiness? Naah. Now it's pursuit of permission.

You have to get a permit to build your home.

You have to get a permit to fill in a low spot in your yard because it might be a wetland.

You have to get a federal permit to have contact with any migratory wildlife. Migratory wildlife is legally the property of the United States. You can get sent to federal prison for feeding the Canada geese visiting your local park.

The idea is to protect the environment and its wildlife. But sometimes the wildlife won't cooperate.

A boating company on the Pacific coast had for years offered whale watching tours, and then Congress made it illegal to come in contact with gray whales. The boat company operators told Congress they would be glad to keep their distance, but the whales insisted on rubbing up against the boats so the people could reach out and pet them.

Whales like people more than environmentalists like people.

Greedy Capitalists

Why is it that some African countries have done an excellent job of conservation while others are plagued with poachers?

Is it a lack of police to shoot the poachers?

It's more like a lack of brains.

Kenya has a national park and nature preserve system that's a bureaucratic morass. Wildlife is a hands-off experience. No hunting. No disturbing the wild animals. And they have a poaching problem that's out of control. It's not just the big ivory trade shooting big tuskers for their big front teeth.

As human settlement encroaches on wildlife habitat in Kenya, people come into conflict with wildlife—mostly elephants. Elephants like to get into the gardens and farms of the settlers. The settlers want to eat their own crops and not feed them to elephants. So the settlers shoot the elephants. They call them poachers. Stiff fines and imprisonment. Terrible problem and it won't go away.

Just down the road in Zimbabwe, they have a national park and nature preserve system that's a capitalist's dream, with fewer bureaucrats.

They have the same problem with settlers encroaching on wildlife habitat. But they don't have anything like the poacher problem in Kenya.

Why? When the elephant herds increase beyond the nature preserve's capacity, they send the surplus outside to the hunting pool, and charge trophy hunters a nice fee, which helps pay for managing the national parks.

Hmm. Why didn't Kenya think of that?

This is an FBI raid!
Give us all your B vitamins!

It was a quiet but busy morning at Dr. Jonathan Wright's Tahoma Clinic. As usual, the doctor was seeing patients from all over the world who came to him for help with various health problems. A highly experienced M.D., he is a leader in natural healing techniques, including intravenous B vitamin therapy.

Suddenly an army of flak jacket-clad invaders smashed through the door brandishing automatic weapons. They terrorized the staff and patients, rifled through files, took papers and equipment—and seized all his injectable B vitamins.

The federal government has never charged him with anything. Dr. Wright sued the government to get back his property.

What was it about those B vitamins that was so dangerous? Were they laced with cyanide? Was Dr. Wright secretly spiking them with heroin? Were patients dying and getting sicker?

No. Patients were improving better than they had with more traditional therapies.

The sin of the B vitamins was that they had no preservatives. Dr. Wright imports them because many patients are allergic to preservatives. The Food and Drug Administration has not approved vitamins in the U.S. without preservatives. So the injectables are classified as *drugs*.

It was a drug raid.

Hmm....

Feeding at the Trough

Our government wouldn't do something as stupid as to give taxpayer money to environmental groups that then spend the money to lobby Congress into giving them more taxpayer money.

Or would they?

Yep, you guessed it. Federal agencies have given environmental wackos millions of your dollars through one government grant or another. Here is a short list of your tax dollars at work:

The Nature Conservancy (1994)	$28,167,119
World Wildlife Fund (1993)	$7,228,199
Ducks Unlimited (1994)	$6,177,725
World Resources Institute (1993)	$3,184,511
Peninsula Open Space Trust (1994)	$3,000,000
Community Environmental Council (1993)	
	$1,598,022
Conservation Fund (1994)	$1,484,251
Sierra Club Legal Defense Fund (1993)	$1,296,350
Save the Redwoods League (1993)	$1,267,000
African Wildlife Fund (1992)	$974,813
National Audubon Society (1994)	$707,038
Center for Marine Conservation (1993)	$680,289
American Humane Association (1994)	$517,753
Trust for Public Lands (1994)	$511,197
Environmental Defense Fund (1993)	$411,123
Defenders of Wildlife (1993)	$384,396
Inform, Inc. (1993)	$309,482
Greenbelt Alliance (1991)	$154,000

Just Who's Endangered Here?

The Hill Country of Central Texas is a rural paradise. So, of course, environmental wackos covet it.

But it's all owned by small farmers and ranchers and in the little towns, by home owners and family businesses.

Now, how does a clever environmentalist pry that land loose from the folks who have lived there and loved it for generations?

Bingo! I know! Let's use the Endangered Species Act!

A member of an environmental group writes a letter to the U.S. Fish and Wildlife Service saying, "Hey, I think the golden-cheeked warbler lives around here. Don't you think we ought to add it to the Endangered Species list?" That's all it takes.

A bureaucrat in Washington, D.C. says, "Hey, great idea! We'll set up a new office in Austin and hire a lot of people and expand our empire."

So they do. And pretty soon they start telling ranchers to stop brush control along their fence lines. Doesn't matter that the cedar brush grow so strongly that it tears up the fences and lets the cows out. Those trees might grow up to be nesting sites for the little birdies.

Then the Bureaucratean Beast declares 33 counties in Central Texas as "Critical Habitat" for the little bird. Now you can't do anything with your land. In 33 counties.

Why does this remind us of King George III?

To Own or Not to Own?

If the leaders of the Sierra Club, the Wilderness Society and the Nature Conservancy were stranded on a desert island, who would survive?

We would.

There would be three fewer thieves trying to nationalize our property rights. But why do they want the government to take all our land in the first place? Sheesh!

Even the village idiot has figured out that what everybody owns, nobody owns. Eco-group leaders aren't so sharp. You know what happens when an environmental leader picks his nose, don't you?

His head caves in.

Just like the former Soviet empire. Private property was illegal there. Great incentive for the workers. It ended up just like the joke that Soviet workers told each other for years: They pretend to pay us and we pretend to work.

The best pay is to be able to own a place of your own. A home of your own, that's the American dream. And eco-freaks spend their donations and fancy foundation grants trying to turn your home into your government's place.

Look what the ban on property rights did for the Soviet environment. Chernobyl. The thickest factory smog in the world. The most polluted rivers.

And here in the U.S. we've done an outstanding job of cleaning up our messes. But it's never good enough for the eco-freak.

He wants the government to take it all.

The Bureaucratean Beast

How many American natural resource workers does it take to change a lightbulb?

One hundred. One to change the bulb, and 99 to apply for the job.

Where the government goes to help manage your land, unemployment is the major growth industry.

Take the redwood region. Back in 1968, the Sierra Club demanded a 90,000 acre Redwood National Park in Northern California. Congress gave them less than half what they wanted.

So, in 1978, they came back for the rest of it.

Now, in 1968 the bureaucrats had promised that the new park would create a tourist boom of more than 900,000 visitors a year. By 1978, the actual number was 35,000, making Redwood the least visited National Park in the system.

The bureaucrats had also promised that loggers put out of work by the new park would receive funds for retraining and job placement. By 1978, not a dime had showed up.

The timber industry said a park expansion would put 1,200 forest and mill workers out of a job. The Sierra Club said it would *only* be 250.

So, how did Congress react when the Sierra Club wanted the failed park expanded? They expanded it. Took nearly 50,000 acres of prime timberland away from the timber companies. Actual job loss by 1979: 1,734.

Q: Does the Sierra Club have herpes?

A: It's screwed enough people to get anything.

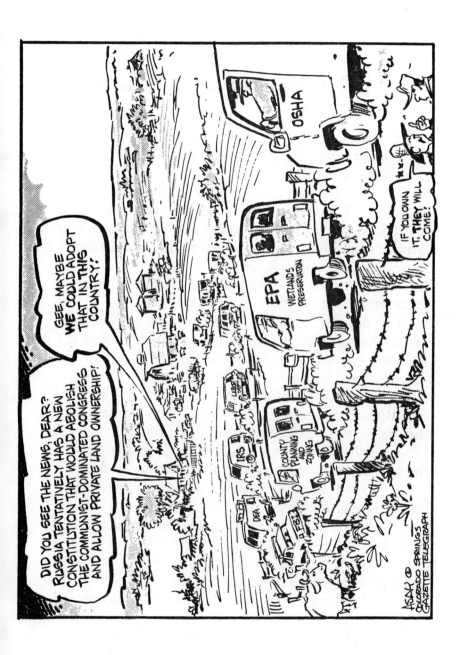

Fair? Bureaucrateans? Hah!

There are two classes of people in the world: Those who divide the world into two classes and those who do not.

Bureaucrateans divide the world into two classes: 1) Eco-freaks who like Big Government, and 2) Redneck radical stupid beer-belly dumbass violent greedy Nazi Pinko Fascist Commie baby-whale-killer murdering raping polluters.

The hapless Average American sees a bureaucratean on TV or in a hearing and, seeing two ears, is deluded that the bureaucratean will listen to both sides of an issue. The citizen does not notice the relative size of the ears. He who sees only half the problem will be buried by the other half.

So, in the public interest, here are the Laws of the Bureaucratean. Take this list with you to public hearings, the court room, the voting booth:

1) If there isn't a law, there will be. And it will be passed against YOU, not against the eco-freak.

2) In case of doubt about some new regulation, make it sound convincing.

3) No matter what occurs, an eco-freak will say it happened according to his pet theory.

4) When embarrassing facts appear, eco-freaks drop the subject to zero importance.

5) Adding two years to the permit delay period will kill any project.

6) Do not believe in miracles—rely on them.

7) If miracles don't happen, fake them.

The Lawyers' Full Employment Era

What's brown and black and looks good on a lawyer?

A Doberman pinscher.

How can you tell the difference between a dead lawyer and a dead skunk in the road?

There are skid marks in front of the skunk.

Why don't sharks eat lawyers?

Professional courtesy.

Lawyer jokes are legion.

Our good friend William Perry Pendley, president and chief legal officer of Mountain States Legal Foundation, told us that as soon as we published his book *It Takes A Hero* he began to introduce himself as an author instead of a lawyer.

We asked him why.

"There are no author jokes."

The reason there are so many lawyer jokes is the old rule, Under any system a few sharpies will beat the rest of us.

Under the U.S. system, environmental lawyers can stop anything because they've beat the rest of us with the principle, Nothing will be attempted if all possible objections must first be overcome. They know how to use the media to argue against anything you want to do. They get Legislation By Headline. They know you can't argue with a man who buys ink by the barrel.

Under the most rigorously controlled conditions, lawyers do as they damn well please. To us.

Contradictions Galore

Walt Whitman wrote in *Leaves of Grass*:
Do I contradict myself?
Very well then, I contradict myself.
I am large. I contain multitudes.
Poetry is a wonderful place for this attitude, but it usually has a few drawbacks in public policy.

America is dependent upon foreign petroleum supplies. The green gang screams bloody murder when we exert military force to protect our foreign oil supplies. It's American imperialism, genocide, and worse.

But how did we get so dependent upon foreign oil?

Well, who was it that refused to allow exploration in 17,000 promising acres of the 1.7 million-acre Arctic National Wildlife Reserve in Alaska? The green gang, of course. They yelled that greedy multinational oil companies would get rich devastating our sacred wildlife. They carefully hid the fact that only a tiny fraction of the refuge had oil under it to be drilled. Or that new technology could develop it with little disturbance.

And who cut off all possibility of drilling for U.S. oil on our continental shelf? The green gang, of course. They lobbied Congress to outlaw American oil from offshore rigs, preventing us from using our own rich oil supply.

The green gang has sabotaged every energy initiative industry has taken to use U.S. oil.

Who's fouling their own nest?

They Made Us Many Promises, And They Never Kept But One. They Promised to Take Our Land And They Took It.

Sioux Chief Sitting Bull is reputed to have spoken those haunting words. And settlers from the United States did indeed enter the traditional Sioux dwelling place and turn it into more United States. The same with all the rest of this vast land we today call the United States.

The conflict over Native American rights remains a trail of broken agreements with the government.

Move over again, Sitting Bull. Now it's the settlers that have the same problem. It took the government a while to get around to it, but they're taking our land, too.

First in the 1950s to create Minute Man National Historic Site in Concord, Massachusetts. The eco-freaks who backed it in Congress said it wouldn't affect private property, but bureaucrateans eventually took hundreds of homes to turn into a park.

At least the government paid for those homes.

Now they've figured out a way to take your land without paying for it. They call it a wetland. There's a law against filling "the waters of the United States." You might be surprised to find that your back yard is "the waters of the United States" if rain puddles there more than two weeks in a row during one year.

Or, by now, maybe you wouldn't be surprised.

Public Land

Government knows best.

When the government gets into the land-owning business, they *really* know best. They start telling *you* how to do it on your own land.

There's this one little catch: The government isn't trying to make a living with its land and you're trying to make a living with yours.

You want your land to be productive. The government wants its land to be politically correct.

So they tell you how to make your land more like government land. Stop farming, stop ranching, stop building houses for people, stop expanding your business place. In short, STOP.

And what do they do with their own land? The Interior Department's management of Mount Lassen Volcanic National Park is a wonderful example.

There was this beautiful lodge for overnight guests with a little store and restaurant at Manzanita Lake at the end of a long national park road. Park visitors loved it for many years. Don Hummel, a Lassen park ranger turned concessioner, had built the rustic stone structure with his own hands.

But eco-freaks decided the lodge brought too much traffic, so they tore that beautiful place down. Then, a few years later some eco-freaks noticed there was nothing at the end of that road, so they sent out a fund raising letter to build a new visitor center at Manzanita Lake.

The easiest way to find something you lost is to buy a replacement, hmmm?

Risk versus Benefit

It used to be people just did what they needed to do. Now you have to apply to OSHA first.

The Occupational Safety and Health Administration will tell you what you're doing wrong. And particularly if you work in the environment.

Congress passed the OSHA law because the American public demanded it. It was for worker protection. It was against greedy capitalists.

Everybody cheered.

For a while.

OSHA wasn't supposed to hurt business. There were supposed to be safeguards built into the law to allow reasonable flexibility.

It didn't work out that way because the bureaucrateans administering the law saw to it. It is impossible to make anything foolproof because fools are so ingenious.

OSHA hasn't increased workplace safety, but they've sure made a lot of silly rules that cost a pile of money for little result.

Then the pubic realized that those freedoms they had taken for granted weren't quite so free anymore.

If the people in a democracy are allowed to do so, they will vote away the freedoms which are essential to that democracy.

OSHA reform?

If it ever appears, it will come from below, from the grassroots. The player holding four aces never calls for a new deal.

Grazing

Grazing is one of those wonderful issues that politically correct environmentalists love.

The public knows virtually nothing about ranching. Less than 1 percent of us ever even lived on a ranch, much less understands the grazing fee issue. So you can tell the public anything.

Here's what the PC crowd says: Hey, some of those ranches are on public land! That land belongs to everyone, and these damned greedy capitalists shouldn't be subsidized by grazing fees that are lower than the going market price of grazing on private land.

Wow! That sounds right, doesn't it?

It's not.

Ranchers with federal grazing permits own most of the value of their ranch to begin with, so they *should* pay lower grazing fees.

Ranchers on federal land have to own a "base commensurable" ranch big enough to winter their whole herd in order to get a grazing permit. So the *rancher* owns some of that "federal" land—why should he pay a market price for what he already owns?

Ranchers on federal lands own the water that rises there because the states, not the feds, have jurisdiction over it. Why should the rancher pay a market price for what he already owns?

Same with the roads, fences, corrals, stock watering ponds, cattle chutes, barns, bunkhouses, ranch houses, and all other infrastructure on the ranch.

Only an eco-freak would demand that you pay for what you already own.

Job Killers, Freedom Killers

A recession is when your friend loses his job.
A depression is when you lose your job.
A disaster is when environmentalists convince the government to protect nature from all jobs.

We've talked about the spotted owl and the 30,000 Pacific Northwest timber workers sent to the unemployment lines by an environmentalist lawsuit.

We've talked about the farmers and ranchers of the Central Texas Hill Country being told to stop everything because of the endangered golden-cheeked warbler.

Have you heard about John Poszgai, who got put in jail for cleaning up a stinking mess in a Pennsylvania sewer drain field behind his small business and got put in jail for disturbing "the waters of the United States"?

Or have you heard about Bill Ellen, the environmental designer who created a series of duck ponds for a rich Wall Street trader's hunting club and got put in jail for disturbing "the waters of the United States"?

Or Ocie Mills, who added sand to his already filled lot in Florida and got put in jail for disturbing "the waters of the United States"?

It's called the Wetlands Regulations. Congress didn't write them. A closed-door session of environmentalists and bureaucrats wrote them. Now federal marshals with guns will make you obey. On your own property. Bow down, America.

What Was The American Revolution About?

A little rebellion now and then is a good thing.
A certified wild-eyed revolutionary said that.
It was that hot-tempered redhead, Thomas Jefferson,
in a letter to James Madison dated January 30, 1787.

Today's popular rebellion against our huge and
oppressive federal government draws spasms of fright
from environmentalists. They fear their carefully-
clenched fist of government command-and-control
might loosen its grip around our throats a little. They
call anyone who fears or hates our federal government a "radical" or a "terrorist."

Well, a radical once predicted, "If the principle
were to prevail of a common law [i.e., a single gov-
ernment] being in force in the United States...it would
become the most corrupt government on the earth."

That's exactly what the eco-freaks are trying to
do to America today. Jefferson was right again. (He
wrote that in a letter to Gideon Granger on August 13,
1800.)

What are we to do? Simply lie down and tell
the environmentalist bureaucrats, "Okay, walk all
over me. Take my home, take my land, take my life"?

We'll probably object.

Are we "terrorists"? Of course not.

Are we "radicals"? The dictionary says radical
means *of the root*, getting back to the roots or funda-
mentals of things. Hmmm.... Tommy, what do you
think?

They Did What?!

Think about this: The European settlers came here and built their homes and farms and ranches.

They fought nature to carve out a place for their children, clearing forests, draining swamps, killing predators.

Their children tamed nature with an industrial society for their children, building cities, building roads for new modes of transportation, improving agriculture.

Their children built a technological society for their children, making higher education widely available, developing mass media, using computers.

And *their* children? Their children made it illegal to drain swamps with wetlands regulations, illegal to cut forests with fancy lawsuits—and they reintroduced predators in the very heartland that got rid of them on purpose.

What did the predators do, once reintroduced?

They predated.

Some on local cows. The cow owners didn't think much of that, so they shot the predating wolves. Under the laws passed by the settlers' great grand-children, that was a felony. Wolves are endangered and the Endangered Species Act provides for $50,000 fines and a year in prison for each offense.

So a federal bureaucrat comes to one of these ranchers and proposes to put him in jail. The rancher calls the county sheriff, who proposes that the bureaucrat go back to his office. The bureaucrat goes.

What did the rancher think about the great grandchildren who made ranching a felony?

He was heard to mutter contemptuously under his breath, "City kids."

Sweet Land of Liberty

"That government is best which governs least."
A lot of folks think Thomas Jefferson said that.
He didn't. The first place this noble sentiment appears in print is in Henry David Thoreau's *On the Duty of Civil Disobedience*, first sentence.
But we like it anyway.
It expresses the feelings of a free people. It is, of course, the bane and horror of politically correct environmentalists. Which is another reason we like it. We especially love the delicious irony that it was said by the environmentalists' own darling, the frog of Walden Pond himself. Think they'll disown Thoreau?
What an eco-heresy he spoke! Imagine the Environmental Protection Agency governing less! Not telling you what to do with your home, your job, your money, your life! Could you stand it?
Eco-freaks couldn't. Less power over you? They can't let that happen. Less control over you? Not a chance. You might—gasp!—USE something.
And that would be The End of Nature, Doomsday, Ragnarök, Götterdämmerung, Kaput, Bye-bye.
If the eco-freaks get their way, and our government governs most, we'll all be deported to the Moon or Mars for using natural resources.
Maybe Thoreau's follow-on is the right way to go. He also said, "That government is best which governs not at all."
Imagine that!

Pesticides and Pests Decide

Environmentalists are the nation's Number One Crop Pest.

They do everything they can to sabotage pest control. They do everything the can to stop the use of pesticides.

And they're very good at it. Just look what they've done with the debate over pesticides: The very word PESTICIDE now has a bad sound to it. You don't like to see it, you don't like to say it. It sounds negative, nasty, dangerous, poison, deadly, creepy, ugly—well, you get it. When you make people flinch from a legitimate word like that, you clearly control the debate.

Pesticide means PEST KILLER. Pests are things that harm people. Killing pests is a good thing for people. Things that kill pests might also be dangerous for people. Some pesticides are. Some aren't.

But any substance, natural or artificial, is dangerous in a large enough dose, and harmless in a small enough dose. The dose is the poison. An early scientist named Paracelsus discovered that fact, so it's named after him, and called Paracelsus' Law. The dose is the poison.

Eco-freaks complain about pesticide residues on fruit and vegetables. They're in such small doses they are harmless. About the same as the natural pesticides vegetables produce to protect themselves.

But tell that to an eco-freak. Zero Risk is their motto. Regardless of the cost—or actual danger.

Really, should pests decide?

Big Business Funds
Big Environmentalism

In environmentalism, the Golden Rule applies: Who has the gold rules.

If you produce corn and you could convince government to create a new market for it by law, wouldn't you do it?

Well, it's easy to make ethanol from corn. And it's easy for Congress to mandate the use of ethanol in your gasoline to make it less polluting. And it's easy for a big agribusiness outfit like Archer Daniels Midland, the nation's largest food ingredient processor, to donate a few thousand buck to the Democratic Party.

But Archer Daniels Midland also backs eco-groups such as the American Farmland Trust ($35,000 in 1989), which buys up valuable farmland and peddles it to the government for nature preserves so no competitor will be able to buy it. That keeps up the price of land owned by Archer Daniels Midland.

Think of all the other big businesses that give money to eco-groups:

The Nature Conservancy gets money from the corporate foundations of Amoco, Arco, Ashland Oil, Borden, Burlington Northern, Cargill, Ford Motor Company and many others.

The National Audubon Society gets big bucks from the foundations of Alcoa, Ford Motor Company, General Electric, H.J. Heinz, Procter & Gamble, others.

Most big eco-groups get big money from big business. They have the gold.

Conservative or Liberal?

Conservatives think that all environmentalists are watermelons: Green on the outside, red on the inside.

Liberals think that all environmentalists are avenging angels: Striking down evil polluters with the Sword of Justice.

There are holes in both theories.

Conservatives are overoptimistic about the intelligence of some environmentalists. For one thing, it takes a little brains to be an eco-socialist watermelon. You have to pronounce all these long technical terms like "gimme" and "I want that," and, yes, they can manage that just fine.

But it's the abbreviated acronyms that trip them up, especially T.A.N.S.T.A.A.F.L. It means "There Ain't No Such Thing As A Free Lunch." An eco-socialist can't wrap his tongue or his mind around that one.

Liberals, too, are a bit too enthusiastic about enviros. Being on the take from evil polluters seems a little strange if you're supposed to be smiting them with that big sword.

But if you're the Wilderness Society, you're even stranger: You have this big multimillion dollar investment portfolio—odd in itself, since this money supposedly came from members who thought they were paying to save wilderness—and you invest in Caterpillar, Cummins Engine, 3M, Illinois Tool Works and McDonalds, among others.

Hmm.... Bulldozers, diesel engines, mines and fast food. Green on the outside, gold on the inside.

Viewsheds

You've heard of watersheds. They're a physical feature of the land that's like a basin draining toward the sea. They shed water from higher places to lower places.

People like to protect them for good reason: we get water from them.

Now get ready for the latest eco-freak fad: Viewsheds.

Never heard of a viewshed? They're an imaginary feature of the landscape that's like a painting facing a viewer. They shed views from prettier places to uglier places.

Eco-freaks like to protect them because they can stop all human activity by claiming it will pollute the viewshed.

Now, there may a certain merit to the viewshed concept, say, inside a national park. You go there for the view. You don't really want a brick wall around the Grand Canyon to keep you from falling in. (The Park Service built one anyway, but it's only knee height if you're 10 feet tall.)

The rub comes if you want to protect a viewshed where the viewer is *outside* the national park and the view is shed on the viewer from *inside* the national park. Now you can stop everything outside national parks.

Then what if the view is somebody's farm and it gets shed on somebody's home?

The visual pollution control cops will be there fer shure.

Rewilding America

Imagine Denver before the white man got there and built a city.

Imagine the mountains, valleys and coasts of California without human settlement.

Imagine the Midwest's farms and fields growing wild in tallgrass prairie, all trace of man's hand eradicated. Not even Native Americans living there.

You might not have to imagine very hard if some of our far-out eco-freak contingent gets their way.

The Cenozoic Society, co-founded by Dave Foreman (one of the co-founders of the ecoterrorist outfit Earth First!), among others, has proposed the Re-Wilding of America.

The "Wildlands Project" is a modest proposal to depopulate a third of the United States, that's all. Most of the Great Plains and the West would become off-limits to human entry. Everything would be torn down and the landscape restored to its original condition.

Like most such modest proposals, the folks who live in the other two-thirds probably wouldn't mind much. Until they found all the roads and highways torn up and the roadbeds restored to their pristine condition.

And until they tried to find Grandma in Denver and Uncle Bob in Omaha, who would be relocated to—somewhere.

Don't bother looking in the phone book for them. There won't be any phones.

Fox in the Henhouse

What happens when the Chief Logger's job is given to someone who hates logging?

Gee, let's see if we can figure that one out.

Loggers will have a tough time of it?

Good guess.

The U.S. Forest Service is landlord of a big chunk of that One-Third Of The Nation's Land the government so proudly owns. (Why does a supposedly capitalist nation have more land in government ownership than East Germany had when it was communist?)

With all that rich timberland, the U.S. Forest Service has historically been the government's head logger. Part of the reason Congress gave the President power to proclaim forest reserves back in 1891 was to assure a steady timber supply as the federal lands were disposed of to actual settlers. Providing timber to the highest bidder, until recently, was the major purpose of the U.S. Forest Service.

Then the eco-freaks started infiltrating the outfit. At first it was a few new college graduates from the 1970s whose professors told them logging was bad. Then it was higher level bureaucrats who believed no logging should be allowed on federal land.

Finally, the job of Chief of the U.S. Forest Service was handed to one Jack Ward Thomas, not known for his love of logging and regrowing trees.

So now the U.S. Forest Service doesn't log any more. So why is there still a U.S. Forest Service?

Practicing Environmentalism Without a License

The eco-freak crowd has always banked on P. T. Barnum's saying, "There's a sucker born every minute."

How else can you account for the hot air about hot air? Global warming is still a wannabe. Even so, already we've passed laws to get rid of CFCs in our car air conditioners and refrigerators, among other Clean Air Act improbabilities.

Environmental scientists who have warned about global warming all seem to obey Finagle's Creed, which goes, "Science is Truth. Don't be Misled by Facts."

They use what's called "computer modeling." You put a bunch of numbers in the computer, you program it to act like the real atmosphere, and you believe the results you get.

Trouble is, nobody knows how the real atmosphere acts, so anything you put in the program is educated guesswork.

When they take their conclusions around to other environmental scientists, nobody sees the mistake.

But the first objective scientists that walks by with unsolicited advice see the mistake immediately.

"Hey, dummy, this is a computer model. You made up the facts to begin with. It can't even predict the weather tomorrow morning."

On this basis we pass laws.

The Church of Gaia

The more we see of environmentalism, the more we hear people comparing it to a religion. Here are some famous comparative religious views about life so you can decide for yourself:

Taoist: Shit Happens.

Confucian: Confucius says: Shit Happens.

Buddhist: This shit is only an illusion.

Zen Buddhism: What is the sound of shit happening?

Hindu: This shit has happened before.

Islam: If shit happens, it is the will of Allah.

Judaic: Why is this shit happening to me?

Catholic: Shit happens to you because you deserve it.

Protestant: Let shit happen to someone else.

Jehovah's Witnesses: I've seen shit happen and I'd like to tell you all about it.

Mormonism: When shit happens, the Stake wants ten percent.

TV Evangelism: I truly belieeeve shit happens.

New Age: Let's take off our clothes, form a circle, and chant about this shit.

Scientology: Can you recall any earlier similar shit?

Rastafarian: Let's roll up this shit and smoke it.

Agnostic: Are you sure this is shit?

Atheist: I don't believe this shit.

Environmentalist: This shit will kill everything.

Wise User: Let's fertilize the garden.

Reporter assigned to cover shit: "Thank God I'm not religious!"

It Just Growed

Has your car air conditioner been wimping out on really hot days? Need a little more freon to pep it up? Maybe a pound and a quarter?

Sure. No prob.

So you take old junky into the car shop. You tell them, "Hey, fill 'er up with freon and check the gas." They say, "Sure," and you go for lunch.

You come back and look at the bill.

$50.00.

Okay, freon is a little pricey, but what the hey, you got your car all nice and cool, right?

Wrong.

Joe, the mechanic you've known and trusted for ten years, has just flushed all the freon out of your air conditioner and left it empty.

"Had to do it," he says. "Needed more than a pound of freon. It's the law. EPA will shut us down if we don't do it."

You yell, "But wait! My air conditioner doesn't work at all now!"

Joe says calmly, "EPA says air conditioning isn't a necessity. You want cool, you have to replace the whole system."

"The whole thing? All the equipment?"

"Yeppers. It's the law."

"How much will that cost me?"

"For your old junker, $600. Plus coolant."

"What?"

"Have a nice day."

The Blond Leading the Blond

Every day is Blond Day for an eco-freak.

Skepticism is not environmentalism's forte.

Give 'em a good doomsday story and they'll swallow it whole, no thought, no investigation, no suspended judgement. Just *gulp!*

Like electric power lines causing cancer. Eco-freaks believe it because their eco-icons said so. So what if nobody who got cancer from electric power lines can be found. The facts don't matter.

If an eco-authority like that famous pesticide scientist, Dr. Meryl Streep, says Alar is bad for kids, then Alar is bad for kids. So what if no record of anyone being harmed by Alar can be found? A screen star who repeats stuff from the Natural Resources Defense Council just *can't* be wrong, dahling.

If they scream, the media will come.

If the media catches cold, liberal politicians sneeze.

Doesn't matter if it's all baloney.

It's like Voltaire said about God, if eco-horror stories didn't exist, it would be necessary to invent them.

Now just because environmental group (A) puts the apple orchardist community (B) out of business in order to save children (C) from Alar, doesn't make A right.

In fact, it calls to mind Mencken's Law: Whenever A annoys or injures B on the pretense of saving or improving X, A is a scoundrel.

(H. L. Mencken, *Newspaper Days.*)

Whoa Thar!

Do environmentalists have fun?

Only at funerals.

How many speeds does an environmentalist have?

One speed: Stop.

Do environmentalists believe this is the best of all possible worlds?

No, they know it.

What do environmentalists think of Murphy's Law ["If anything can go wrong, it will."]?

Murphy was an optimist.

The Environmentalist's Final Solution:

If you can't eat it, screw it, fake it, or get rid of it, regulate it.

What are the Ten Commandments of Environmentalism?

1) Forget the good things in life and dwell only on the bad.

2) Disregard the feelings and rights of others.

3) Act like your opinions are indisputable facts.

4) Leave no good deed unpunished.

5) Insist that you are exceptional and entitled to be obeyed.

6) Never overlook a slight or forget a grudge.

7) Cultivate a consistently gloomy outlook.

8) Put an excessive value on nature.

9) Feel sorry for everything except people.

10) Don't laugh. Ever.

Reality Happens

Our friend John McClaurghy of Vermont is an astute political observer who understands eco-freaks better than the average bear.

McClaurghy's Iron Law of Zoning: When it's not needed, zoning works fine; when it is essential, it always breaks down.

In 1974, when McClaurghy was chairman of the Planning Commission of Kirby, Vermont, population 230, the town had zoning but absolutely no need for it since nobody was moving there and no development pressure existed.

But consider the zoning the feds impose on anything private in or near federal land. If you want to open a motel or ski area or tourist attraction in the middle of nowhere, the paperwork will cost more than the construction and occupy more space.

If, on the other hand, the federal government wants to build a new bureaucrat nest in Washington, D.C., they don't provide parking because they want you to use public transit, they don't care how many homes or apartments they condemn to clear the way for their new palace, and they have no idea what it will actually cost.

McClaurghy's Law of Public Policy: Politicians who vote huge expenditures to alleviate problems get reelected. Those who propose structural changes to prevent problems get early retirement.

Eco-motto: If it jams, force it. If it breaks, it needed eliminating anyway.

Deep Ecology

Eco-guys Bill Devall and George Sessions know how you should act. Here are their non-negotiable demands, quoted verbatim from their book *Deep Ecology*:

1. The well-being and flourishing of human and nonhuman Life on Earth have value in themselves (synonyms: intrinsic value, inherent value). These values are independent of the usefulness of the non-human world for human purposes.

2. Richness and diversity of life forms contribute to the realization of these values and are also values in themselves.

3. Humans have no right to reduce this richness and diversity except to satisfy *vital* needs.

4. The flourishing of human life and cultures is compatible with a substantial decrease of the human population. The flourishing of nonhuman life requires such a decrease.

5. Present human interference with the nonhuman world is excessive, and the situation is rapidly worsening.

6. Policies must therefore be changed. These policies affect basic economic, technological, and ideological structures. The resulting state of affairs will be deeply different from the present.

7. The ideological change is mainly that of appreciating *life quality* (dwelling in situations of inherent value) rather than adhering to an increasingly higher standard of living. There will be a profound awareness of the difference between big and great.

8. Those who subscribe to the foregoing points have an obligation directly or indirectly to try to implement the necessary changes.

Natural Resources

Want to do a double take?

Okay. The liberal kid in Chuck Asay's great cartoon isn't wrong.

Wow! What's that again?!

The liberal kid is right. In a sense, your checkbook *is* a natural resource. Sure, it's man-made, a human artifact, the product of thought and work, made from raw materials found in nature, extracted, exchanged and manufactured into a final usable form.

A *resource* is something to use, a source of supply, an item that can be exchanged or traded off for something else.

In that sense, resources are *all* man-made.

A tree is just a natural *object* when it's standing in a Jurassic forest millions of years before people existed. It is not a natural *resource* because it's not a source of supply available for exchange or trade-off.

Resource is a word correctly applied ONLY to things used as a source of supply. If it isn't an actual or potential source of supply, it's not a resource, it's something else. In most cases, just an object.

So, in a sense, the liberal kid is right. That check book *is* a natural resource. He just wants to use it for his own purposes without the burden of paying its original producer and owner.

The modus operandi of the eco-freak.

Sound Science

Bad news drives good news out of the media.

Everybody knows that, and it's no different when the news is about science. Sure, science is supposed to be about the truth.

If truth doesn't get good ratings, it is the first casualty of reporting.

The public isn't much interested in science, so this rule always applies: Pure drivel tends to drive ordinary drivel off the TV screen.

Eco-drivel is the purest form of drivel.

Because the public isn't much interested in science, if it doesn't flash lights or blow up, TV can't handle it.

So unless it is some great catastrophe that can be represented by mangled bodies or fast-moving pieces of stuff, nobody will believe it.

People believe that everything they see on TV is absolutely true except for that rare story of which they have firsthand knowledge.

Media-savvy scientists have figured out The Rules Of The Game:

1) When scientific law is against you, argue the facts of your particular study.

2) When the facts of your particular study are against you, argue scientific law.

3) When both scientific law and the facts of your particular study are against you, call the other scientist names.

Trade-offs

It all costs, so why do they call it the freeway?

Probably nothing offends an environmentalist more than the Americans' love affair with the automobile.

When it comes to cars, eco-freaks have cursed, wept, banned, regulated, jabbed, stabbed and crabbed.

Does the public listen? Not a chance. We know a good thing when we see it.

For us, a car is not just transportation from point A to point B, as it is for the environmentalist. It's fun, freedom, a joyride—words that don't exist in an environmentalist's vocabulary.

In their relentless drive to eradicate the automobile, eco-freaks have insisted on public policy that cars must be more fuel efficient.

The real idea is to make the standards so strict that no car can possibly pass the test. But engineers are a crafty lot, and resourceful.

They keep coming up with lighter materials from which to make cars, more power-easy engines, and a thousand little details to do more with less.

Cars keep getting more fuel efficient.

It drives the eco-freaks crazy.

But that wasn't a long drive anyway.

We Need More Money

If there's anything you can always predict about the Bureaucratean Beast, it's the plaintive cry for more money.

It doesn't matter what the project is or what regulation needs to be enforced.

Administrative costs grow in direct proportion to the expanding universe or something else we can't control. That way they can blame it on the Big Bang. But it doesn't matter, because they're going to keep doing it the way they always have.

The Bureaucratean Beast's Prayer: "O Lord, grant that we may always be right, for Thou knowest we'll never change our minds."

The Bureaucrateans Beast's Standard Replies:

We get appropriations from people who get their names in the newspapers. The public is not made up of people who get their names in the newspapers. Therefore, the public is always wrong.

Don't tell us we should do it better, for to try doing it better means to admit we are presently doing it worse. That could affect appropriations.

When lobbying Congress for more appropriations, sincerity is essential. Even if you have to fake it.

Malpractice makes malperfect. We've been doing it wrong for so long it seems right.

Nothing is impossible as long as we don't have to do it.

Those who are ignorant of history are doomed to repeat their mistakes. Those who know history will find other ways to make mistakes.

We need more money.

Acting Scared

Fear for sale! Nice fresh fear right here!

We got Alarm over Animal Companions! Prevent pets!

Here's some nice Horror over Homes! Zone us to zero!

Have some of our Dread over Desertification! Lop off logging!

Try our newly cooked up Anxiety over Anthropocentrism! Punish people!

You'll love our Dismay over Dams! To hell with hydropower! Forget flood control!

Then there's Panic over Private Property! Prevent personal prosperity!

And, dahling, you simply must have our Fright about Farmers! Ban bug butchering! Gnurture Gnuisance Gnats!

This little number is the next trend, sweetie, so try on our Suspicion of Speciesism! Hammer humanity!

Concern over civilization! Destroy development!

Foreboding about Free Enterprise! Rout the risk-takers!

And we have a nice assortment of direct mail frights: You can Cower, Shrink, Tremble, Quail, Shake, Cringe, Blanch and Start about a wide variety of made-to-order disasters.

Just call Eco-Fright. 1-800-DIE-SOON. Eco-Fright, The *Quality* Fear Merchants.

VISA and MasterCard accepted.

If You Think Big Government Solves Problems, You'll Just Love This Little Bridge I'm Selling

The farther you live from the environment, the more you want to keep others out of it.

The less you have to do with the environment, the more you appreciate it.

Eco-lobbyists know this. They prey on the armchair environmentalist in us all. Show us pretty pictures to excite our sympathy for nature. Show us horrific tales of rape, plunder and burn to arouse our hatred of the culprits. Convince us that Walt Kelly's cartoon character Pogo Possum was right: We have met the enemy and he is us.

Then go to Congress with this mass of seething resentment against ourselves. Show them your big membership numbers. Flood them with angry letters and telegrams and phone calls. Pass laws that stop everything—but incrementally, a little at a time, so it just pushes the limits of political possibility.

When the government has enforced these laws long enough for the economic and human damage to show, deny all responsibility. Claim that the industry you destroyed was declining anyway and that obsolescence, automation or foreign competition killed it. Claim anything that can't easily be proved.

Then convince your members that, since the problem isn't going away, there's not enough government intervention. Pass more laws, etc.

Repeat as necessary.

They're Comin' Tuh Git Yuh, Pilgrim

You haven't been harassed until your federal government has harassed you.

The feds have yet to see any problem, no matter how complicated, which, when two bureaucrats look at it, did not become still more complicated.

If you think you're quietly minding your own business somewhere, a federal agent with a gun will start a confrontation designed to make it look like you were minding the government's business and that you started the confrontation.

Like Dwight Hammond, a rancher in Central Oregon, who grazed his cattle on federal land, but owned the water rights on the federal land.

The feds one day told him he had to keep his cows away from his own water. They threatened to build a fence around his water to keep his cows from getting to his water.

Dwight parked an old bulldozer on the rutted trail to his water. The feds took that as an act of civil insurrection and sent agents to pick a fight with Hammond. They hoped he would lose his temper, show a gun, and they could settle the question of who owned that water then and there. They would just take Dwight to town in a box and that would be that.

Dwight didn't blow his cool, though. He just insisted he owned his water. So they roughed him up, put him in chains and leg irons and threw him in jail.

Your tax dollars at work.

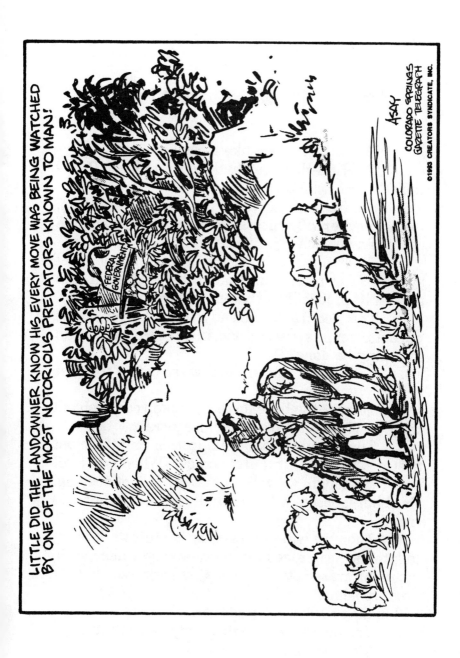

Your Politically Correct Future

Hell hath no fury like a pacifist.

God Him-Her-Itself hath no wrath like a Politically Correct Eco-Freak.

Eco-freaks hate you. They hate themselves, too, so they're *really* miserable. Misery no longer loves company, nowadays it insists on it.

Eco-freaks also insist you believe in their belief system. The more ridiculous a belief system, the greater its probability of becoming government policy.

The Eco-freaks already control a lot of the bureaucracy, as we've seen in these pages. Can anything be done?

Yes, but things will get worse before they get better.

To beat the bureaucracy, make your problem their problem. We're sick of bureaucrats.

That means most of us in this country must first get fed up with bureaucracy. When we've all suffered enough, we will all just get sick of obeying. Even bureaucrats will eventually get sick of bureaucrats.

Then we will get together in our own locales, talk to the people we have been having trouble with, including grassroots eco-freaks, and begin solving our own problems. Localism won't solve our problems, it will make *us* solve our problems.

The bureaucracy will simply be irrelevant. Visualize that!

5
This is a Test
This is Only A Test

If it was a real P. C. Inquisition, you'd be hanging by a strappado from the ceiling right now. For those who weren't around when Friar Torquemada was running the National Testing Service in Spain, a strappado is a torture in which your wrists are tied behind your back and you are hoisted by them, then allowed to fall to the length of the rope. If you are into S&M, this could be considered a fun thing to do. Most of us don't like tests that much. This section of P. C. tests is guaranteed to be slightly less painful.

Consider it something like a high school pop quiz, a little surprise bonus that comes with the book.

Test Your Environmental IQ

Follow these instructions carefully:

1) Read the entire test before answering any questions.

2) Keep track of your answers on a separate piece of paper. Do not write in this book.

3) You may use a calculator when adding up your scores.

4) The one who dies with the most toys wins.

5) The one who lives longer than the winner gets to laugh last.

TEST No. 1 - ANIMAL WISDOM

Test your understanding of the Revealed Truth About Animals (revealed by the gurus of gloom in the animal rights movement). Ten points for each correct answer.

Scores from 1 — 10, Human, all too human; 20 — 30, Stupidity with a human face; 30 — 40, What fools these humans be; 40 — 50, To err is human, to forgive is against our policy; 50 — 60, Four legs good, two legs bad, except for the birds; 60 — 70, Your animal magnetism is a little stronger; 70 — 80, All animals are equal, you're just not *quite* as equal as others; 90 — 100, You animal, you.

Question 1: According to PeTA (People for the Ethical Treatment of Animals), a boy is:
1) a rat.
2) a dog.
3) a pig.
4) all of the above.

Question 2: George Eliot wrote the famous quote, "Animals are such agreeable friends—they ask no questions, they pass no criticisms" in *Mr. Gilfil's Love-Story*. The politically correct view of this quote is:
1) George Eliot was a nice lady who loved all animals.
2) George Eliot was a nasty violent bloodthirsty animal abuser viciously mocking their lack of speech.
3) George Eliot's books should be burned.
4) George Eliot should be burned.
5) Everybody who reads George Eliot should be burned.
6) Everybody should be burned.

Question 3: D. H. Lawrence's advice, "Be a good animal, true to your animal instincts" is:
1) Good.
2) Bad.
3) Impossible for humans.
4) Likely to get you arrested.

Question 4: You are in a lifeboat that has room for only two. You are accompanied by a bright dog and a retarded girl. Who should you throw overboard?
1) The bright dog.
2) The retarded girl.
3) Yourself.
4) All of the above.

Question 5: Human beings should stop being speciesist, and refrain from eating all other life forms.
1) True
2) False
3) What?

Question 6: Botanical Companions should have the same rights as Animal Companions, so why isn't there a Plant Rights Movement like the Animal Rights Movement?
1) We're working on it.
2) The vegetarians don't like the idea.
3) I didn't like eggplant parmigiana anyway.
4) Why are they hugging trees instead of slugs?
5) I wouldn't want my dog dating one of them.

Question 7: Mineral Companions should have the same rights as Plant Companions and Animal Companions, so why isn't there a Mineral Rights Movement like the Plant Rights Movement and the Animal Rights Movement?
1) We're working on it.
2) The dietary supplement companies don't like the idea.
3) I never eat chalk anyway.
4) I wouldn't want my Dahlias dating one of them.

Question 8: This is supposed to be a quiz on Animal Wisdom. How come there are so many questions off the subject?
1) The copy cat refused to think up any more animal gags until we increase her Meow Mix ration.
2) It was getting late at night.
3) The dog ate my homework.
4) The dog ate the copy cat.
5) I wouldn't want my rocks dating one of them.

Question 9: Who will be the next President of the United States?
1) The King of Colorado
2) The Prince of Philadelphia
3) The Duke of Delaware
4) Kim Basinger
5) I'd rather date a dolphin

Question 10: If animals have rights, how come none of them are lawyers?
1) All lawyers are animals, stupid.
2) They communicate their demands to animal rights activists through telepathy.
3) They communicate their demands to animal rights activists by cellular phone.
4) Animal rights activists made the whole thing up, and have no idea what animals want.
5) Kim Basinger.

Answers:
1) 4.
2) 6.
3) 1. Don't argue.
4) 2. We know because an Animal Rights guru said so.
5) True. Animal Rights activists first.
6) 2.
7) 4. Our Dahlias have led a very sheltered life.
8) There is no correct answer, so you can't make a perfect score. HaHaHa.
9) 5. Some animal rights women have had sex with dolphins. Their only complaint about their well-endowed and randy lovers was that they had a hard time keeping the postcoital cigarette lit.
10) 5. Well, we just have animal instincts about Kim Basinger.

TEST No. 2 - ENVIRONMENTAL THOUGHT QUIZ

RECOGNIZING POLITICALLY CORRECT ENVIRONMENT WHEN YOU SEE IT

Question 1: What game is this?

"I'll wager one 300-foot setback on your lot."

"I'll see your setback & raise you two asphalt-paved urban hiking trails crossing your lot."

"I'll see those setbacks & trails, & raise you 2 golf courses waiting for construction permits."

"I'll see the setbacks, trails, & golf courses, & raise you four $1.4 'illion' worth of articulated buses containing 3.2 passengers (one of whom is an Alpo-American who rides each free test run with his dog to keep warm in winter, cool in summer, dry in the rain).

"I'll see all of that, & trump with a $6.7 'illion' paved bicycle lane carrying 12 bicycles/day alongside the $14 'illion' light rail system free test run carrying 4 people (& possibly the dog) in one of the 40-passenger cars that roars by your home 6 times an hour."

"Call."

(End of this inning).

Name of the Game:

A: Environmental Hockey (Puck Poker)!

B: Land Grab!

C: Break the Taxpayer!

D: Power to the Pee Pull!

E: Other _____.

Correct answer is worth 10 points.

WHERE ON EARTH?

Question 2: What country is this?
In which of the following countries of the world do you need a permit to plant a garden?
1. North Korea
2. United States of America
3. Sweden
4. Cuba
5. Russia
6. Holland

10 points for each correct answer.

Question 3: What country is this?
In which country of the world does the government get to decide the color of your front door?
1. People's Republic of China
2. Vietnam
3. United States of America
4. Peru
5. Zimbabwe
6. Monaco
7. Grand Fenwick
8. Erewhon
9. All of the above

10 points for each correct answer.

MULTIPLE GUESS:

Question 4: Why do these countries do that?
1. This decision has great impact on the environment. It might kill everything.

2. Bureaucrats need more work to do and we wouldn't want idle hands becoming the devil's workshop.

   3. The Constitution requires it. I read a book about it once. By an environmentalist.
   4. Does government need a reason?
Correct answer is worth 10 points.

MULTIPLE GUESS:

Question 5: Where in the world are we now?
   In which country of the world do laws protect the rights of people to assemble on weekends & say whatever they want, and then go to the outdoors and do whatever they want in the environment?
   1. Cuba
   2. North Korea
   3. Iraq
   4. United States of America
   5. Ecotopia.
Correct answer is worth 10 points.

MULTIPLE GUESS:

Question 6: Why do these countries do that?
   1. Because people need to be protected from government.
   2. That's not the only right that's protected from government interference.
   3. What do you mean, interference?
   4. That's ridiculous, why would government care about assembling & talking?
   5. Do they have weekends in North Korea?
   6. What do you mean, protected from government?
   7. I thought we had to ask if it was OK to do stuff like that.
   8. Is Iraq somewhere in North Dakota?

9. Are any two people in Cuba together enough to assemble?
Correct answer is worth 10 points.

MULTIPLE GUESS:

Question 7: Who would want to do that stuff anyway?
1. National Audubon Society.
2. Sierra Club.
3. Earth First!
4. National Republican Women's Club.
5. Dittoheads.
6. Wilderness Society.
7. Weathermen.
8. Animal Liberation Front.
9. PLO.
Correct answer is worth 10 points.

ESSAY QUESTIONS:

(Answer any 3 — Use 25 words or less for each essay)
1. Explain the environmental impact of front door color choice.
2. Explain the environmental impact of garden permits.
3. Research & report on which pages of YOUR county's planning documents these two items appear.
4. Open essay: Choose your favorite crucial environmental detail. Research and report on its origins, impact and rationale. Remember, 25 words or less.
100 points for any answer.

Answers:

1) E. Any answer roughly equivalent to "A stupid game" gets 10 points.

2) 2.

3) 3. Or 8. Grand Fenwick is the country that defeated the United States in *The Mouse That Roared*. Or 9. *Erewhon* is Samuel Butler's utopia in which an animal rights vegetarian cult ate only cabbages certified to have died a natural death.

4) 4. Of course not.

5) 4. Within limits.

6) 8. We think Iraq has been spotted about 70 miles southwest of Fargo, North Dakota.

7) Any answer is correct. We thought we would make up for that lousy trick we played on you in scoring test one. It's possible to get double a perfect score on this one. Just not likely.

TEST No. 3 - NAME THE SPECIES QUIZ

Question 1: What species is Walt Disney's Pocahontas?
   1. *Homo politicalis correctus.*
   2. *Luvsus animalus.*
   3. *Moneymakia boxofficinalis fantasticus.*
   4. *Watta crok,* v. *retrohistoricus.*
   5. *Who's Walt Disney?*

Question 2: Name the genus, species and subspecies of any one of the three largest newspaper companies that give money directly to environmental groups:
   1. *Tempus, New York Citiensis arborchompum.*
   2. *Postum, Washingtoniana grahamcrackeria.*
   3. *Tempus-Reflectus Corporationæ (Tempus, Los Angelenoxius fakeus).*
   4. *What is this? I can't even read English!*

Question 3: What species is the Sierra Club?

    1. *Homo antieconomicus.*

    2. *Crotalus horridus, lawyer.*

    3. *Hikeus solitaria, goawayeverybody.*

    4. *Skrewia all.*

    5. *With its increasing extremism and declining membership, how about "endangered"?*

Question 4: What species hides behind the protective coloration of protecting nature then leaps out and kills jobs?

    1. *Nationalicus Wildlife Federationalis.*

    2. *Nationalicus Audubon Socialisticus.*

    3. *The Wilderness Socialisticus.*

    4. *Greenpiece.*

    5. *How can you distinguish between such similar species?*

Question 5: Identify the mating call of The Nature Conservancy and related species:

    1. *Sendmoney! sendmoney! sendmoney!*

    2. *We sell private land to the government!*

    3. *We develop our land but you can't develop yours!*

    4. *Gimmee government grants! gimmee! gimme!*

    5. *Tonsomoney! Tonsomoney! Tonsomoney!*

Question 6: Identify the color variations of the:

    1. Environmental Defense Fund

        a. Greed and gold.

        b. Gold and greed.

        c. Ford Foundation gold.

    2. Friends of the Earth

        a. Greed and gold and clout.

        b. Gold and greed and clout.

        c. Clout and greed and gold.

Question 7: Identify the reproductive strategies of:
1. Natural Resources Defense Council
    a. Rockefeller money.
    b. Mellon money.
    c. Pew Charitable Trusts money.
2. World Wildlife Fund
    a. Rockefeller money.
    b. Mellon money.
    c. Pew Charitable Trusts money.

Question 8: Identify the defensive strategies of:
1. Greedpeace
    a. Blame it on the Wise Use Movement.
    b. Blame it on the Wise Use Movement.
    c. Blame it on the Wise Use Movement.
2. Earth Island Institute
    a. Blame it on the Wise Use Movement.
    b. Blame it on the Wise Use Movement.
    c. Blame it on the Wise Use Movement.

Question 9: Identify the predatory strategies of:
1. National Parks and Conservation Association
    a. Direct mail.
    b. Phony doomsday messages.
    c. Revenge on industrial civilization.
2. U.S. Public Interest Research Group
    a. Door to door soliciting.
    b. Phony doomsday messages.
    c. Revenge on industrial civilization.

Question 10: Identify the natural allies of eco-groups:
1. Big money foundations.
2. Big money corporations.
3. Big money land sale to the government.
4. Big money investments.
5. Big money government grants.

Scoring Test 3:

1. 1 thru 4 are correct. Not right, correct. There's a difference.

2. 1 thru 3 are correct. Ditto.

3. 1 thru 5 are correct, but debate has arisen about 3. *Crotalus horridus* is the timber rattlesnake, and *lawyer* is the subspecies. Representatives of the rattlesnake genus have protested being associated with the Sierra Club, lawyers and this book.

4. 1 thru 4 are correct.

5. 1 thru 5 are correct, but 1 is the only call the public is likely to hear. The species seeks privacy in its dens before venting the calls in 2, 3 and 4. Although call 5 is clearly observable, the species behaves as if it were the call of its opponents in the Wise Use Movement.

6. Environmental Defense Fund: 3.
   Friends of the Earth: 1 thru 3.

7. Question 1: 1 thru 3. Question 2: 1 thru 3.

8. Do we need to tell you?

9. All answers correct.

10. All answers correct.

TEST No. 4 - AGRICULTURE POLICY QUIZ

Question 1: Select one answer to complete the following sentence:

"The opportunity to sell directly through co-operatives has made the difference between continuing to farm & knuckling under to:

1. land developers."

2. oppressive taxation."

3. Bill Gates and Microsoft."

    4. rapacious regulatory takings."

    5. environmental impact requirements."

    6. the Mafia."

Question 2: What's a farm?

    1. No fair. We didn't have that in high school.

    2. I think it's where they make puppies.

    3. The 4H Club meets there.

    4. Isn't it something you fill out?

    5. It's where farmers live.

Scoring Test 3: Agriculture doesn't make any difference anyway, so give yourself a perfect score.

TEST No. 5 - CONSTITUTION SHORT QUIZ

Question 1: Which Constitution specifically guarantees the right to own private property?

    1) Russia.

    2) United States of America.

Question 2: U.S. Constitution, Bill of Rights:

    1) Is this sentence long enough?

    "Congress shall make no law."

Scoring Test 4:

    1. 1. The U.S. Constitution makes no guarantee of any kind for the right to own private property, only to be compensated when the government takes it away, yet the new Constitution of Russia, ratified after the fall of the Soviet Union, does, in the strongest terms.

    2. The sentence is complete as it stands.

TEST No. 6 - TERRORIST MULTIPLE CHOICE

Question 1. WHICH OF THE FOLLOWING is a terrorist or terrorist organization?
1. Earth First!
2. Sierra Club
3. Unabombers Anonymous
5. Rush Limbaugh
6. Jean-Paul Sartre
7. Phil Donahue
8. BATF
9. Animal Liberation Front

Question 2: IDENTIFY WHICH are left or right-wing terrorists (some may terrorize both):
[ ]L [ ]R 1. Unabomber
[ ]L [ ]R 2. Earth First!
[ ]L [ ]R 3. BATF
[ ]L [ ]R 4. Republican National Committee
[ ]L [ ]R 5. Dittoheads, inc.
[ ]L [ ]R 6. Weathermen
[ ]L [ ]R 7. AARP
[ ]L [ ]R 8. SDS
[ ]L [ ]R 9. The Pink Panthers
[ ]L [ ]R 10. None of the above.

Question 3: Environmental laws & mitigation fees add 40% to cost of new housing.
1. True.
2. False.
3. Equivocal.
4. Those figures have not been checked.
5. It's just a statistic.

Question 4: Who said, "It's 10 pm, do you know where your government is?"
1. Thomas Jefferson.
2. Bill Clinton.
3. Joe Lunchbucket.
4. Isn't it everywhere?

Question 5. Who said: "Give me government or give me death?"
1. Patrick Henry.
2. John Henry.
3. Henry David Thoreau.
4. Henry Adams.
5. Adam Ant.

Question 6. Who said: "That government is best which governs least."
1. Thomas Jefferson
2. Henry David Thoreau.
3. Bill Clinton.
4. Joseph Stalin.
5. Ramses II.

Scoring Test 5:
    1. 9. ALF actually made it to the FBI's top 10 most wanted domestic terrorists. Not that some of the others haven't tried.
    2. 10. They're all off the list now.
    3. 1. It's OK. Poor people don't buy new housing.
    4. 3. Who else would worry about it?
    5. 2. John was Patrick's crazy half-cousin, who had a speech impediment and thus became the darling of the politically correct in Revolutionary times,

whose organizations preserved this deathless cry of courage from one generation to the next so that we here in the modern era may wonder at its bravery and inspiration.

     6. 2. No, Tom didn't say that. Bill who? Joe had it backwards and Ram Baby, well, he'd have to ask his Temple Priests to take the omens before he knew what he thought. But you won't find it carved on his tomb.

TEST No. 6: DEBATE SOCIETY QUIZ

DEBATE #1: WHAT'S IT ABOUT, CHARLEY?

A: RESOLVED: The environmental movement is about saving the environment.
B: RESOLVED: The environmental movement is about wealth, power, and control.

DEBATE #2: AMERICA

A: RESOLVED: "Those beggars are fleecing me. It isn't the America I signed up for."
B: RESOLVED: "We want an environmentalist in every garage and a permit in every pot. It is only right to worship trees & sacrifice people."

DEBATE #3: GOVERNMENT

A: RESOLVED: "Hating government is not a good thing. We propose to institute 'Love Your Captor' week.
B: RESOLVED: "Hating government is OK. We had a Revolution to prove it, and those people hadn't even heard about bureaucratic subversion of civil liberties."

DEBATE #4 ASSEMBLING

A: RESOLVED: "Earth First! is doing too much assembling during the week, while..."
B: RESOLVED: "The Audubon Society is doing too much assembling on the weekends. Can we compromise?"

DEBATE #5: BOMBING

A: RESOLVED: "The Unabomber: We can't figure out who's doing this. It's probably the right wing bombing itself."
B: RESOLVED: "Eco-terrorists are law abiding saints who never destroy property or hurt people. Just because the Unabomber talks Deep Ecology doesn't mean there's any connection. Of course, the most imaginary relation of a wise use leader to somebody who knows somebody who likes militias is absolute proof of guilt that they bombed the Oklahoma City federal building."

Scoring Test 6:
    1. A. Of course, honey.
    2. B. You're politically correct.
    3. A. Keep a civil tongue in your head
    4. Tossup. Either is correct.
    5. A. Of course the right wing bombs itself. The left wing would never bomb the right wing.

Final Scoring:

If you've answered any question, you automatically flunk the test.

Go back and read the first instruction. It says:

"1) Read the entire test before answering any questions."

So this was really a test of how well you can follow instructions.

It had nothing to do with the politically correct environment.

Like the rest of this book.

Laugh.

It's a joke.

Now you can enjoy the Merril Press **Politically Correct** series of silly, tasteless, thought-provoking, hilarious and downright philosophical humor books. Each is 180 pages, 3 quality paperbacks priced at $14.95 each.

Politically Correct Hunting, written and illustrated by Ken Jacobson. Of course, there's no such thing as politically correct hunting, so Ken Jacobson takes a romp through the cherished beliefs of animals rights activists while sharing his many years of real outdoor experience as a hunter and guide.

Politically Correct Environment by Alan Gottlieb and Ron Arnold, with cartoons by Chuck Asay. Two leaders of the Wise Use movement poke a whole lot of fun at stuffy, self-righteous eco-pests, with political cartoons by one of America's boldest newspaper cartoonists.

Politically Correct Guns, by Alan Gottlieb. A take-no-prisoners sortie deep behind enemy lines among the gun control crowd, jabbing them with their own hypocrisy and stupid actions, written by a leader of the gun rights movement.

If you have enjoyed **Politically Correct Environment**, you'll want these other exciting titles from Merril Press.

Trashing the Economy: How Runaway Environmentalism is Wrecking America, by Ron Arnold and Alan Gottlieb, 670 pages, paperback, $19.95.

It Takes A Hero: The Grassroots Battle Against Environmental Oppression, by William Perry Pendley. 346 pages, paperback, $14.95.

Storm Over Rangelands: Private Rights in Federal Lands, by Wayne Hage, 288 pages, paperback, $14.95.

Stealing the National Parks: The Destruction of Concessions and Public Access, by Don Hummel, 428 pages, hardcover, $19.95.

Ecology Wars: Environmentalism As If People Mattered, by Ron Arnold, 182 pages, paperback, $14.95.

The Wise Use Agenda, edited by Alan Gottlieb, 168 pages, paperback, $9.95.

Mail to: Merril Press, PO Box 1682, Bellevue, WA 98009
Telephone orders: 206-454-7009   FAX orders: 206-451-3959